A GENEALOGICAL HISTORY
OF THE
ULSTER O'NEILLS

By PETER J. O'NEILL

*Dedicated to My Wife, Bridie
and Son, Peter J. O'Neill
and Daughters, Margaret, Patricia and Teresa*

The O'Neills of Ulster like most of the chief families of Ireland, are descended from Milesius, the Celtic King of Northern Spain. Several centuries before the birth of Christ, the Celts, a tall, blue-eyed, blonde and red-headed race of people, swept through Europe as conquerors. One branch settled in Spain, where King Milesius died. After his death a famine wasted the land, and King Milesius' sons with their mother Scotia, and their followers decided to seek a new land. Hearing from their Druids of an island flowing with milk and honey, the most western island of Europe, they set sail with sixty ships, filled with their vassals, women, children, soldiers, artisans, laborers of all kinds, under forty chiefs, commanded by the sons of Milesius, **Hermon, Heber, Ir** and **Amergin.** After a stormy voyage off the coast of Ireland which separated the ships, the Milesians landed in two divisions, Hermon on the coast of Leinster and Heber on the coast of Munster. Heber soon after met the Tuatha de Danians who were the ruling race in Ireland then. Their army, commanded by their Princess Erin was defeated by Heber, who soon after joined his brother Hermon. The united forces met up with the main army of the Tuatha de Danains on the plains of Tailton, commanded by their three Princes. In the battle that followed, the three Tuatha de Danains Princes were slain with their principal officers and their army destroyed. This victory gave the island empire to the Milesians.

The brothers, Hermon and Heber, as chiefs of the colony divided the island between them. The other brothr Ir died during the landing and Amergin was a Druid. Heber took Munster and Hermon took Leinster. They gave Ulster to Ir's son, Heber-Don with some other chiefs, leaving Connacht to the Firbolgs, who helped them in the war with the Tuatha de Danains. The fiefs and lordships were distributed among the other chiefs according to rank and merit. The two brothers, Heber and Hermon ruled Ireland together for one year. Through the ambitions of Heber's wife, who wanted to be Queen of all Ireland, forced her husband to declare war on his brother, **Hermon.** In the battles that followed, Heber was slain and **Hermon** became the **first Monarch of Ireland,** which he ruled for the next thirteen years. Fifty-eight High Kings (Ard-Reighs) of Hermon's race ruled over Ireland before St. Patrick, and fifty more of the same race ruled Ireland after St. Patrick, mostly UI Niell.

The remote ancestor of the O'Neills of Ulster, was **Niall** the great or **Niall of the nine hostages,** who became Ard-Reigh High King of Ireland, A.D. 379. He seems to have conquered parts of Britain and France. On one of his excursions in France, he captured the boy Patrick, who later became St. Patrickk and converted the Irish to christianity. He was called Niall of nine hostages, from his nine tributary Kingdoms—Ulster, Munster, Leinster, Connacht, Britain, Pict, Dalriads, the Saxons, and the Morini, a people in France near Calais.

Marching with a victorious army to free the Celtic natives of France from Roman rule, he was assassinated by the King of Leinster as he rested on the banks of the river Leor in France. Niall was married first to Inne. His second Queen was Reigneach, a daughter of the King of Britain, by whom he had eight sons, Eoghan, Laeghaire, Conal Crimthann, Conall Gulban, Fiacha, Main, Cairbre, and Enda. Niall Mor was the 125th Monarch of Ireland and 87th of the O'Neill No. I pedigree. He was succeeded by his nephew, Dathy.

After Niall Mor's death, his son, Eoghan (Owen), led his three younger brothers, Conall Gulban, Enda and Carbery, with their followers into the northwestern portion of Ulster, now Donegal, which was then inhabited by the Fir-Dorma, a Firbolg race. The brothers quickly overran and captured the great Firbolg stone fortress known as the Grianan of Aileach, a huge circular fort, supposedly built one thousand years before the birth of Christ. Its ruins still stand on a high Hill overlooking Derry City. Owen made it his headquarters. From it, his descendants were able to overawe all of Ulster, and thus was born the Over-Kingdom of Aileach (Ulster).

During the next five centuries, twenty-five of its Kings were also High Kings of Ireland. Owen was the first King of Aileach. From him, the **O'Neills of Ulster** were descended. His brother, Conell Gulban is the ancestor of the O'Donnells. The descendants of Enda and Carbery sank into obscurity. Their memory still remains on in Tir-Enda in Donegal and the Barony of Carbery in Sligo.

The Kingdom of Aileach was composed of the present Counties of Tyrone (land of Owen), Donegal, Derry, parts of Armagh, Fermanagh and Sligo, but it overshadowed all of Ulster. The descendants of the four sons of Niall, who remained in Ulster were called the **Northern Ui Niall**. The descendants of the four sons who remained in the Kingdom of Meath were called the **southern Ui Niall**. The two branches of the descendants of Niall the great, from the fifth to eleventh century, succeeded peacefully to the High Kingship of Ireland. One reigned from the northern U-Niall and the next from the southern Ui-Niall.

This peaceful succession continued until the Ui-Niall were overthrown by Brian Borou in 1002. This destroyed the unity of the country, through the ambitions of the Provincial Kings who each wanted to be High King.

The term Ui-Niall is a kin-name, not a surname. The surname O'Neill can only be applied to the descendants of **Niall Glunduf**, King of Aileach and High King of Ireland. He was killed fighting the Danes near Dublin in 919 A.D. St. Patrick, when he was in Ulster, decided to visit Aileach Nead, the home of Prince Owen, who he then converted to Christianity, with all his household and vassals. St. Patrick spent forty days in Aileach, and was treated with great honor and respect by Prince Owen, who gave him several grants of land to build his churches on.

Prince Owen was married to a British Princess and was the father of ten sons. He divided Tyrone among them, giving their names to different districts. Sixteen of Owen's descendants were High Kings of Ireland and a great number Kings of Ulster. Five of his sons left posterity, carried down to the present time. Prince Owen, No. 88 on the pedigree, reigned forty years as king of Aileach, dying in 465, it is said from grief on the death of his brother Conel Gulbin. Owen was succeeded as King of Aileach by his oldest son, Muredeck, who was the ancestor of the O'Neills of Ulster and other families.

Muredeck was married to Erca, daughter of the King of Alba. They were the parents of sons, namely Murkertach Mor McErca, Fredic, Turlough Oge, and Mongan. **Murkertach Mor McErca**, No. 90 on the pedigree became King of Aileach on the death of his father Muredeck, and High King of Ireland in 497.

This is the beginning of the alternate succession between the two branches of the Ui-Niall which was to continue until 1002. **Murkertach Mor McErca** was married to **Duach**, daughter of Tengumba, King of Connacht. He was a reknowned warrior, a winner of many battles. In the early part of his reign, he sent six of his brothers into Alba, where they formed a Kingdom comprising a fourth part of the present Scotland. One of them, Fergus Mor McErca held a part of the present England where he died. Murkertach died in 529 from burns received when his house caught fire. He was a pious Monarch, as several monasteries were established during his reign. He left five sons, Donald, Bouden, Fergus and Fichera.

Donal I, eldest son of Murkertach Mor McErca, succeeded him as King of Aileach. He became the 134th High King of Ireland in 561. He associated his brother, Fergus with him in the Kingship, a war with the Leinster King who tried to be High King, in which the Leinstermen were defeated, in a famous battle at Gabhra-Liffe. They also had wars with the Connacht King. They both died of the plague. Donal had three sons, Eocha, Hugh and Colga. **Eocha** became King of Aileach on the death of his father in 566 A.D. He became High King of Ireland as **Eocha XIII**. He associated his uncle, **Baoden** in the government.

During his reign, the monastery of Erach Dune was founded in Galway. He and his uncle were killed at Glengiven by Cronan, son of Tigernach, Prince of Kienachta.

His brother then became King of Aileach and High King of Ireland in 605 A.D. as **Hugh IV**, surnamed **Variodnach**, he was renowned for his justice. His reign was disturbed by wars in which he was successful. He died at Tara after a seven year reign. Eocha XIII had a son, **Mailfitrace** who died before he became King of Aileach, leaving a son **Maildivine**, who was married to a Ticonnell Princess. He became King of Aileach and died in 706 A.D. He was the father of two sons, **Fergal** and **Adam**.

Fergal became King of Aileach and later High King of Ireland. During his reign, plunderers from Britain began raiding the countryside. Gathering his army, Fergal defeated them in a fierce battle at Cloch-Mionari in Ulster. He died in 722 A.D., leaving two sons, **Hugh** and **Niall**. **Hugh** became King of Aileach and High King in 734 A.D. as Hugh V. He was an enlightened monarch, but he died in 738 A.D. His brother Niall succeeded him as King of Aileach. Niall became High King in 763 A.D., surnamed Freasach, from the three Showers that fell at his birth—a shower of Honey, a shower of Silver and a shower of Blood.

Ireland had great peace during his reign, but suffered from famine and earthquakes. After a reign of seven years, he abdicated and retired to a monastery. where he lived for another eight years. Niall Freasach was succeeded by his son, **Hugh**, surnamed Oirnigh, in the Kingdom of Aileach. Hugh became High King of Ireland in 797 A.D. During his reign the Danes began making bloody attacks in various parts of the land, burning towns and looting churches and monasteries with great savagery.

During Hugh VI's reign, the famous Priory of Kells was built, which gave the nation the great historic Books of Kells. Hugh VI died in Tirconnell after a 22 year reign leaving two sons, Niall Caille and Mailduin.

Niall Caille succeeded his father, Hugh VI as King of Aileach and was elected Ard-Reigh or High King in 833 A.D. During his reign the Danes made great efforts to conquer the country. They had by then established themselves in the principal seaports such as Dublin, Wexford, Waterford and other smaller places. They began plundering the countrysides and building fortresses called Danes Rathes, which were constructed of earth, round in shape and built on hills, into which they could retire when attacked by the Irish. Many of them still remain in various parts of the island.

Niall Caille, having quelled a revolt of the inhabitants of Fearkeal in the Kingdom of Meath, marched against the Danes and he defeated them in a great battle near Boire in Ulster. He afterward defeated them in another battle in Tirconnel. Marching south to attack the Danes of Wexford and Waterford, he was accidentally drowned in the River Caille, now Callen County Kilkenny in 845 A.D. Its from that river he got his name Caille. He left left two sons, Hugh and Flaherty. **Hugh** succeeded him as King of Aileach. Hugh was married to Maolimure, daughter of Kenneth, King of the Scots. Hugh helped his father-in-law to defeat the Picts and become King of all Scotland. He became High King in 863 A.D. as Hugh VII. He marched against the Danes and defeated them in a great battle on the shores of Lough Foyle, killing several thousand of them with forty of their Chief men.

Later with one thousand horsemen, he was victorious over a mixed army of five thousand Danes and Irish insurgents, killing a great number of them. **Hugh VII** called Fionlia, died December 12th, 879 A.D. in Donegal, leaving two sons, **Niall Glundubh** and **Donal**. Niall Glundubh became High King of Ireland in 916 A.D., succeeding Flan-Sionna, who was of the southern Ui Niall.

One of Niall's first acts was to re-establish the fair of Taiteen which had not been held for some time. In 917; he marched against the Danes, who were devastating Ulster with fire and sword. He defeated them with great loss. He then marched against the Danes of Wexford and Waterford to prevent them from ravaging Leinster. In 919 A.D., he led an army against the Danes of Dublin and was mortally wounded. He was married to Gromlith, daughter of the Ard-Reigh, Flan-Sionna. There is an old poem which represents her as standing by the grave of her husband and commanding a monk not to set his foot on that clay. She died in religious retirement in 948 A.D.

Niall Glundubh was the 170th monarch of Ireland. From him the surname O'Neill is derived. Niall Glundubh was succeeded in the Kingdom of Aileach by his son, **Murkertach**, surnamed **Murketach of the Leather Cloaks**, from the cloaks worn by his soldiers. He was the Roydamna or heir to the throne of Ireland. Murketach was a renowned military leader, winning many victories over the Danes, which gave him the name of the Hector of Western Europe.

With an army of one thousand men of special valor, he began the circuit of Ireland for High King Donough II. The provincial Kings usually gave hostages to the High King. When he began his reign, Murkertach started out by seizing Sitric, King of the Danes; next Lorcan, **King** of Leinster; then Callaghan,

King of Cashel Munster, who had joined the Danes in an invasion of the Kingdom of Meath and Ossory in 937 A.D.

Murkertach next proceeded to Connacht, where the king, Connor, son of Teige, came to meet him. He then returned to Aileach, carrying those Kings with him as hostages; and for five months he feasted them with knightly courtesy, then sending them to the Ard-Reigh, High King Donough in Meath.

The Danes still continued to conduct bloody raids against the churches and monasteries. In one of those raids, they met Murkertach in the district of Lecale, where he defeated them in a great battle, killing eight hundred of them. He again defeated them on the shores of Lough Neagh, killing twelve hundred of them. After many victories over the Danes, he was surprised and slain by Belcaire, Lord of the Danes in 941 A.D.

On the death of Murkertach, his son, Donal and grandson of Niall Glundubh, was the first to assume the name of O'Neill, became King of Aileach or Ulster. He succeeded to the High Kingship of Ireland in 956 A.D. During his reign, the Danes made many plundering raids on the Kingdom from their seaport towns of Dublin, Wexford and Waterford, even inducing the people to revolt in an attempt to overthrow the government and were successful in Leinster and Connacht. Donal defeated the Danes and put down the revolts in Leinster and Connacht. After more successes against the Danes, Donal died in Armagh after a reign of twenty-four years. He had three sons, **Malichie**, **Murkertach** and **Hugh**.

Malachi II succeeded his father, Donal O'Neill as High King of Ireland in 980 A.D. He was called Malachi the Great. He was a valiant and warlike prince. He began his reign by attacking the Danes and fought the memorial battle of Tara, at which the Danes suffered a disasterous defeat with the loss of five thousand men and many of their chiefs, including Reginald, the son of their King Aulaf.

After his victory over the Danes at Tara, Malachi marched into their territory of Fingal, which surrounded Dublin, and laid seige on that city, which he captured after three days, freeing two thousand Irishmen who were prisoners there, including Donal-Claon, King of Leinster.

The Danes, through Malachi's victories, were forced to abandon all the territory they controlled from the Shannon east to the sea and to acknowledge Malachi as their over-King. However, the Danes, having received large reinforcements from their home country, again began hostilities, despite the treaty they had signed with Malachi, with the pillage of churches and destruction of the countryside.

Malachi II then attacked and defeated them in two battles,

under their Chiefs, Tomor and Carolus. He is still remembered in song and story as the Malachi that wore the Collar of Gold won from the proud invader.

It was unfortunate that after those victories over the Danes that Malachi gave himself up to pleasure, neglecting the welfare of the nation and allowing the Danes to grow stronger. He was forced to abdicate his title of Ard-Reigh or High King in 1002 A.D. by Brian Borou, King of Munster. After Brian Borou's death at the battle of Clontarf in 1014 A.D., Malachi II again became High King (Ard-Reigh). He repaired and rebuilt many of the churches and monasteries destroyed by the Danes. He granted pensions for the support of poor orphans in several towns.

When the Danes of Dublin, with those that escaped from Clontarf, began plundering the country again, he called the O'Niells of Ulster, who came with their troops. They then marched toward Dublin, defeating the Danish army at Fordvey. They then captured Dublin, crushing the Danes and giving the city up to plunder. Malachi built a well-known monastery near Dublin and several other institutions. He died in September 1022.

After Malachi's death, the **O'Neills** retreated into Ulster and Ireland was never again united, except for brief intervals down to the present time.

Of the 44 High Kings that ruled Ireland from the 4th to 11th centuries, of the race of Niall of the 9 hostages, 16 were descended from his son Owen; 9 from his son Conal-Gulban and 19 from the 4 sons that remained in Meath. The line of succession to the High Kingship, regularly alternated from the north to the southern Ui-Neill. The usurpation of Brian Borou destroyed the peaceful succession to the High Kingship and opened up the nation to the ambitions of the provincial Kings, each struggling for the honor of Ard-Reigh. Thus we had the O'Briens, O'Connors, O'Loughlins fighting each other for the title and none of them strong enough to be acknowledged by the entire country, sapping the strength of the nation and paving the way for the Anglo-Norman invasion and another eight hundred years of warfare and English brutality.

The O'Neill's had now returned to Ulster and **Flathartach An Frostain** of the pilgrim's staff, grandson of Donal the Ard-Reigh became King of Aileach in 1019 A.D. He brought an army against the foreigners and took Irish prisoners from them. He made a pilgrimage to Rome in 1030 A.D. and died in 1033. He had four sons, Hugh, Donal, Murehertach, Muredach. **Hugh O'Neill**, oldest son of Flathartach became King of Aileach on his father's death. At that time Ulster was divided into two kingdoms—Aileach and Ulida, which was composed of the present counties of Antrim and Down. Aileach was made up of the seven remaining counties. It would seem that Hugh O'Neill imposed his rule over all of Ulster before he died in 1036 A.D. Hugh had two sons, Donal Roydana or heir to Aileach and Hugh, who was the ancestor of the McSweeneys of Tirconnel. **Donal O'Neill** never became King of Aileach as the McLoughlins who were descended from Donal, a brother to Niall Glunduff, the ancestor of the O'Neill's, seized the Kingship of Aileach during Donal's minority, so that from 1036 to 1166 A.D., the McLoughlins seems to have control of Aileach. One of them for a short period was the Irish Ard-Reigh. Donal O'Neill died a young man. He left a son, Flaherty, who was the father of Conor of the Woods and whose son, Tadhy of the Glen, was father of Murchartac of Moylining. All those princes were styled Roydannas or heirs to Aileach and Ulster. They were also Lords of Telachog, one of the free states of the Kingdom of Aileach. The kingdom was made up of free states and subject states. the free states were not taxed and were usually ruled by relatives of the reigning family.

The relationship between the O'Neill's and the McLoughlins seemed to be fairly good, even though the O'Neills never conceded that the McLoughlins were ever Lords of Aileach until Murchertac of Moylinning was killed by the McLoughlins in 1160. This, after he had waived his own claims to the throne, providing he or his descendants should have their turn to the Kingship. Murchertac was married to a daughter of O'Floinn, who was the ruler of a small state east of the river Bann, known as Ui Thurt. Murchertac O'Neills son, Hugh, called Toinlesy Macaohm was only a child when his father was killed. He was hid by his grandfather O'Flionn to prevent him from falling into McLoughlin's hands. This Hugh O'Neill was still a very young man when he broke down the supremacy of the McLoughlins, after Murchertac McLoughlin, King of Aileach died.

Hugh O'Neill and Murchertac's son, Niall, struggled for the Kingship of Aileach. The contest was resolved by dividing the territory between them, Niall taking the northern half and Hugh taking the southern half, which was roughly the present County Tyrone and parts of the adjoining counties. This arrangement didn't work out, for in 1169, Conor McLoughlin was installed in Hugh O'Neill's place. But Conor was slain by the McCanns at Armagh in 1170 and Hugh O'Neill was reinstated.

In 1171, **Hugh O'Neill** sent a force of men to help Roderick O'Connor, the Ard-Reigh, who was besieging Strongbow and the Anglo-Norman invaders in Dublin. In the same year, he refused to submit to Henry II of England, who had landed in Ireland, and was recognized as sovereign by all the other Irish chiefs. In 1174, Hugh O'Neill marched into Meath with his army, driving out the English settlers up to the walls of Dublin. In 1177, Hugh O'Neill, King of Aileach was defeated and slain by his rival and kinsman, Malachlan McLoughlin. Hugh O'Neill had two sons, Niall Raudh (red haired) and Hugh Meth. Niall Raudh was the ancestor of the O'Neill princes of Tyrone and Hugh Meth, the ancestor of the O'Neill princes of Clanaboy.

The Clans subject to the O'Neill Princes of Tyrone in the 12th century were:

1. The O'Neill Princes and Kings of Aileach.

2. O'Kanes, Chiefs of Cinnachta and Colrein in Derry - a branch of Cinel Owen.

3. O'Connors, Chiefs of Cinnachta before the Kanes.

4. McDermott Chiefs of Bredach, the parishes of upper and lower Moville.

5. O'Gormley Chiefs of Cinel Moen in Donegal.

6. Magh Itha, a district partly in the Barony of Rapho Donegal and the Barony of Tirkeenan Co. Derry. The Chiefs were:

1) O'Boyle, 2) O'Quin and O'Kinny, 3) O'Brody, 4) O'Hogan of Carnabrack, 5) O'Hagan of Tullachoge, 6) O'Donegan, 7) McMurrough, 8) O'Freil, 9) McRogers, Chiefs of Telach Ambuik and Muniter Barn district in the Barony of Dunganon and Strabane, 10) O'Kelly, Chief of Coreighan Barony of Dungannon, 11) O'Terney, 12) O'Keirnan, Chiefs of Fermanagh, 13) O'Dubhdan, 14) O'Hamells, 15) O'Egans, Chiefs of Telach Cathedra Dubaiuba, 16) O'Maelfethartigh and O'Hosey, Chiefs of Cinel Tighemnugh, 17) O'Cooney, 18) O'Baolhagalloch, Chiefs of Clan Fergus, 19) O'Morrough and O'Mellan, Chiefs of Aedh Fanaugh and 20) McFaochmach, Chief of Cinel Ferudhugh, South Tyrone.

Also, 21) O'Haermin, Chief of Ferudhugh, North Tyrone, 22) Clan Maelgimerich, 23) McTully of Muniter Tauth Laigh, 24) O'Hainbitas of Ui Seeum, 25) O'Clearehan of Hy Fichercia, 26) O'Quin, Chief of Moy Lugid, 27) O'Carlan, Chief of Clan Dermot, 28) O'Bradley, 29) McCloskey, 30) O'Devlins, Chief of Muniter Devlin, near Lough Neagh, 31) O'Looney, Chief of Muniter Looney Mountains in Tyrone, 32) O'Connellian, Chief of Croch Tullach County Tyrone, 33) O'Donnellys, Chief of Ballydonnelly, County Tyrone, 34) O'Neary, Chief of Cinal Naens, 35) O'Laverty, Chiefs of Cinel Moen, 36) O'Murry in Derry. 37) McShanes, a name anglicized to Johnston, a clan in Tyrone, and 38) O'Genewes, hereditary Bards of the O'Neills.

PRIVILEGES OF THE KINGS OF AILEACH

The Tributes of the King of Aileach and his stipends were:

1. **A hundred sheep and a hundred cloaks, a hundred cows and a hundred hogs, from Cuilian Traidhe.**

2. Thirty hogs, thirty cows and thirty wethers from Tuatha Ratha.

3. 300 hogs, 300 cows and 300 weathers, from the men of Lurg.

4. 300 cows, 300 beeves, 100 tinne from the King of Ui Fiachrach.

5. 100 beeves, 100 cows, 100 hogs and 50 cloaks from the McCarthain.

6. 300 beeves, 300 cows, 300 hogs from Cinachta of Gleann Gleenhin.

7. 10 hundred milch cows, 100 beeves, 50 oxen, 50 hogs from Fir Lir.

8. 100 milch cows, 50 hogs, 50 cloaks from Ui Tuirtre.

9. 100 beeves, 100 milch cows, 50 cloaks from the men of Magh Iothe.

The free Chieftainships of the Kingdom of Aileach were: Tuloch Og, Craebh an Magh Iotha, Innishowen and Cineal Connell. Those states were free from tribute because their Chiefs were of the same blood as the King of Aleach, being all descended from Niall of the Nine Hostages.

Tutha Ratha, a territory in the northwest of County Fermanagh, Chief O'Flanagan; the men of **Lurg**, the barony of Lurg in the north of County Fermanagh, Chiefs Muldoon. **Ui Fiachrach** were seated in the northwest of Tyrone, along the river Derg, comprising the Parish of Ardstraw and some adjoining Parishes.

Ui MacCarthain, now the Barony of Tirkeenan in the west of County Derry. The Cianachta, now the Barony of Keenachta in Co. Derry. **Fir Lir**, now the Barony of Colerain in Co. Derry.

The King of Aileach, when he is not King of Eire, is entitled to sit by the King of Eire at banquets and fairs and to go before the King of Eire at treates, assemblies, councils and supplications. He is entitled to receive from the King of Eire: 50 swords, 50 shields, 50 bondsmen, 50 dresses and 50 steeds, which he allots to the Chiefs of the various small states in his Kingdom of Aileach.

Niall Raudh, No. 112 on the O'Neill pedigree was Prince of Ulster and was married to Nuala O'Connor, daughter of Roderic O'Connor, the 183rd monarch of Ireland. Neil made one attack on the English invaders who were conquering Antrim and Down, and took from them 1200 cows. He died soon after, leaving one son who was known as Brian Catha Duin, then a minor. Niall Raudh was succeeded by his brother, Mugh Meth or Dubh, who was a good soldier. Following in his brothers footsteps, he attacked the English under John DeCourcy, who he defeated killing a large number of the invaders. In 1199, the Anglo-Normans invaded Tyrone but were defeated and forced to withdraw by Hugh O'Neill. In 1201, he went to the assistance of Cathal Crovederg O'Connor, King Connacht, who was dethroned by Cathal Carrick O'Connor, who had the help of the Anglo-Norman Burkes.

O'Neill was defeated and made a prisoner at Ballysodare, County Sligo. When he returned to Tyrone, he was dethroned by the McLoughlins. But he seems to have regained his territory shortly after and expelled the McLoughlins, who returned in 1203 with English help, but were repulsed by the Cinel Owen.

In 1205, Hugh made a treaty with John DeCourcy. In 1208, Hugh attacked the O'Donnells. In 1213, he defeated the English at Carlingford, County Down and burned their castle. He next invaded Meath, driving the English settlers out. In 1224, Tyrone was invaded by the English but were forced to retreat with loss by O'Neill. After that the English made peace with him. He died in 1230, King of Cinnel Owen, a king, who, according to the annalists, inflicted great defeats on the foreigners.

It was Hugh's descendants who conquered 600,000 acres in Antrim and Down from the English, which was named Clanaboy. After Hugh O'Neill's death the McLoughlins again became Kings of Aileach or Cinnel Owen, which they held until 1241, when Donnell McLoughlin was defeated and slain, with 10 of his clan at the battle of Cairmirghe by Brian O'Neill, son of Niall Raudh O'Neill, in alliance with the O'Donnells of Tirconnell.

Brian O'Neill Catha Duin or **Brian of County Down**, 113 on the O'Neill No. 1 pedigree, became King of Tyrone after the battle of Camirghe, which destroyed the power of the McLoughlins, who never recovered from its effect, although they continued on as land owners in Innisowen.

The more than 100 years of internal struggle destroyed the old Kingdom of Aileach. From its wreckage, two new states arose - Tyrone and Tirconnell, who for the next four centuries fought the English tooth and nail until they were finally defeated at the battle of Kinsale in 1602 A.D. The O'Neill's in the line of Brian of Down continued on as Princes of Tyrone until 1607 A.D. when the last Chief Hugh O'Neill, the great Earl of Tyrone fled to Europe. He died in Rome.

Brian O'Neill was a great soldier and a good ruler. He defeated the English in 1250 when they attacked Tyrone, led by Maurice Fitzgerald and again in 1253 when the English were defeated with great loss. After another attack by the English, Brian went after them into County Down and destroyed many of their castles. He was then recognized as King of Ulster. In 1254, he met with Hugh O'Connor, King of Connacht and Taghe O'Brien, King of Thomond. They then formed an alliance and elected Brian O'Neill Ard Reigh or King of Ireland. Brian is reckoned as the 184th Monarch of Ireland. Later in the same year, they met again at Drumkinis on Lough Erne and elected Donal O'Rourke King of Breffiny. In 1258, Brian O'Neill, the new Ard Reigh, with Hugh O'Connor and many Chiefs of Ulster and Connacht, met the English mail-clad Army at Brunderg, County Down. The Irish army who fought without mail were defeated and Brian O'Neill and many of his chiefs were among the slain. Brian was the last Irishman to be elected Ard Reigh. He left two sons, Donal and Niall.

Donal succeeded Brian as King of Tyrone, which was greatly weakened after the battle of Down. Donal was expelled by Hugh Boy O'Neill with the help of the Earl of Ulster, who made Hugh Boy King of Tyrone, but was later expelled by Donal O'Neill. The English Earl of Ulster again expelled Donal and made Niall Culinach O'Neill King.

Nial Culinach was later slain in battle with **Donal O'Neill**, who then became King with his own power. He then expelled the English out of Tyrone. He died in 1325, leaving four sons -Hugh Ryhmer, Brian, John and Cu-Ulida.

Donal O'Neill is remembered in history for his Remonstrance addressed to Pope John XXII, by his attached children, Donal O'Neill Rex Ultoniae, true heir by hereditary right to all Ireland, as well, the Kings nobles and Irish people in general of the same realm.

Donal proclaims the high antiquity of Irish Monarch and the Independence down to the days of Laeri, the first Christian Ard Reigh, from whom Donal derives in direct line. After Laeri, native Kings ruled Ireland till Pope Adrian, on false representations and blinded by English prejudices, handed the dominion of Ireland, de facto, over to Henry II, though he had no right de iure to do so.

Through the oppressions of the English, we are driven to the woods and rocks and fifty thousand of both races have perished by the sword alone in virtue of Adrian's Bull. The English Kings moreover have violated the very Bull and narrowed the bounds of the Church, yet our Bishops are so slavishly timid that they never venture to appeal to your Holiness. The Irish have been depraved, not improved by intercourse with the English, who have deprived them of their ancient written laws and introduced infamous ones such as that no Irishman may sue an Englishman. No man of this race is punished for the murder of an Irishman. Even the most eminent an Irishwoman, no matter how nobe, who marries an Englishman is deprived at his death of her dowery. On the death of an Irishman, the English seize his property, thus reducing to bondage the blood which flowed in freedom from of old.

Further, an iniquitous statute has of late been passed at Kilkenny, forbidding Irishmen to be received in monasteries in English land, and this by counsel of certain bishops, the principal being the Archbishop of Armagh, a person of small discretion and no knowledge. The English in Ireland in the middle nation, differ so widely in their principles of morality from those of England and all other nations, that they may be called a nation of the most extreme degree of perfidy. Lay and cleric, they assert its no more sin to kill an Irishman than it is to kill a dog.

All the land they occupy in Ireland, they occupy by usurpation. By their scheming, they have alienated us from the King of England, hindering us from holding our lands as voluntary tenants under the crown. Aliens from us in language, circumstance and actions, all hope of maintaining peace with them is out of the question. We have made long attempts to obtain legal equality. For example, two years ago, several of our nobles addressed the King through John DeHotham, now bishop of Ely, describing our wrongs and offering to hold our lands directly of the King (according to Adrian's Bull, of which we send your Holiness a copy) or that he should, with consent of both, divide the land between us. But we have no answer from him or his council.

Therefore, if we are driven to fight against both him and our enemies here, we cannot be accused of disloyalty or perjury inasmuch as neither we, nor our ancestors ever did homage to him and his ancestors. All this we verify by the testimony of twelve bishops.

Finally, dispairing of justice, we have called Edward Bruce, a descendant of some of the most noble of our ancestors and by letters patent, have granted to him, our whole right and — for the establishing of justice and equity in the land, which have failed hitherto for want of a proper supreme authority — have constituted our Lord and King by unanimous consent.

May it please your Holiness, then, to sanction our proceedings, forbidding the King of England and our adversaries here from molesting us further or at least enforce from him and them the due requirements of justice.

Pope John XXII's response to the Remonstrance was tepid and disappointing. He informed the contemptible King Edward II of the complaints of the Irish and urged him to carry out reforms according to Adrian's Bull. He then excommunicated friars, mendicants and others who preached rebellion, then issuing another Bull against the adherents of Edward Bruce.

Edward Bruce landed at Larne Harbor with six thousand men. It was a mixed force of Norman-Scottish-Gaelic soldiers. Bruce's first victory was over the local levies of the Ulster colonists under Mandeville and Logan, after several victories over the colonial forces. The Ulster princes urged Bruce to take the Crown. Donal O'Neill renounced in his favor his ancient hereditary right and Edward Bruce was crowned King of Ireland in open air on the hill of Knocknemelan near Dundalk on May Day 1316 in the presence of his Irish allies.

After several more victories over the English, he was finally defeated by a much larger colonial and English army at the Hill of Faughart near Dundalk on October 14th, 1318. Bruce had with him three Thousand Scots and his Irish allies. Edward Bruce was slain with half of his Scots and his head sent to Edward of England. With the death of Edward Bruce, the native Irish alliance fell apart. Nevertheless, it did some good for the native chiefs. The 3 year war ruined the colonial magnates and much of their lands were recovered by the native chiefs.

Hugh Ryhmer O'Neill, No. 115 on the O'Neill Pedigree, became Prince of Tyrone on the death of his father, Donal. He was married to Gromlaith, daughter of the O'Donnell. In the old annals he was called the best chief of his time. He drove out the English from his territory. He made peace with Oreil and Fermanagh in 1339. In 1343, he deposed Niall O'Donnell and made Angus O'Donnell Chief of Tirconnell in his place. His wife Gromlaith died in 1352. In 1354, he defeated a combined force of English and Clanaboy O'Neill's. He died in 1364, King of Ulster. He had three sons - Niall, Brian and Donal.

Niall O'Neill, No. 116 on the pedigree, succeeded his father, Hugh as Prince of Tyrone. He is described by old writers, as pillar of dignity in uniting his own countrymen, exalting the Church and science, distrust of the English and the preservation of his own Principality. The McMahons, McGuires and other minor chiefs of Ulster recognized him as their overlord, giving him hostages. In 1374, he defeated the English, killing several of their knights and a large number of their soldiers. In 1383, he forced the Savages, English settlers in County Down to submit to his Lordship. He burned Carrickfergus, another English settlement. In 1387, he rebuilt Ermaine, the ancient palace of the Clan Rory monarchs of Ulster, destroyed 1,000 years before and bestowed it on the learned men of the country. Hugh Ryhmer had two sons, Niall Oge and Henry Avery or the contentious.

Niall Og succeeded his father, Niall More in 1397. In 1398, he was at war with the O'Donnells and forced them to recognize him as their over-King, which they did. He was already recognized by all the rest of Ulster including the English. Niall Og died in 1402, King of Ulster. He was married to Una O'Neill, daughter of Donal O'Neill. He had two sons - Owen and Brian and one daughter, Una and several other sons not recorded. He was succeeded, not by his son, Owen, but by a nephew, Donal, son of Henry Avery, who was his Tanist.

This Donal was known as Donal Bog or soft. Niall Og's son, Owen became his Tanist and married his daughter. Donal Bog was slain by the O'Cahans in 1432 and **Owen O'Neill** became Prince of Tyrone.

Owen O'Neill, No. 118 on the pedigree, and son of Niall Og, No. 117, was made chief of Tyrone in 1432, after the death of Donal Bog, his cousin. In 1435, Owen defeated the O'Donnells and Brian Og O'Neill, who was competing with Owen for the Kingship of Tyrone. Owen was a great fighter. He attacked the English pale, burned Dundalk and forced the English settlers to pay him tribute. He then proceeded to Longford and through Meath, forcing the English colonists, such as Nugents, Plunkets, Sirbuts and others to pay what came to be known as Black Rent. The O'Connors of Offaly, O'Malloys, McGeoghans, McLaghlins and other Irish clans in Meath gave him their fealty. He visited O'Connor Sligo. After a number of confrontations with the O'Donnells and other chief in which he was mostly always victorious. Owen resigned as King of Ulster in July 1455. He had five sons - Henry, Hugh, Brian Art and Phalem. His sons, **Hugh Art** and **Phalem** founded sub-states under him. **Hugh**, in the **Fews in Armagh** and **Art** the **Clan Art** of **Omagh**.

Henry O'Neill, No. 119, the oldest son of Owen, was installed the O'Neill Prince of Tyrone by the Coarb of St. Patrick, the McGuires, McMahons, O'Cahans and all the O'Neills at Tullaghoge according to the usual customs. Henry was married to Gormely Cavanagh, a daughter of McMorrough, King of Leinster and had issue, Con More Roderic, killed by the sons of Art O'Neill; Tuathal, killed by the Anglo-Normans; Donal, Henry Og and Slain.

In 1458, Henry went with O'Donnell on an expedtion into Connacht. In 1459, he attacked the castle of Omagh and expelled the sons of Art O'Neill into Donegal. In 1462, Edward IV of England sent him a chain of gold and 48 yards of scarlet cloth as a peace offering. He then subdued the O'Cahans, who had declared themselves independent. He banished the Savages out of County Down, then installed Patrick White Lord of Lecale. He conquered the McQuellans of Antrim. In 1482, he resigned his

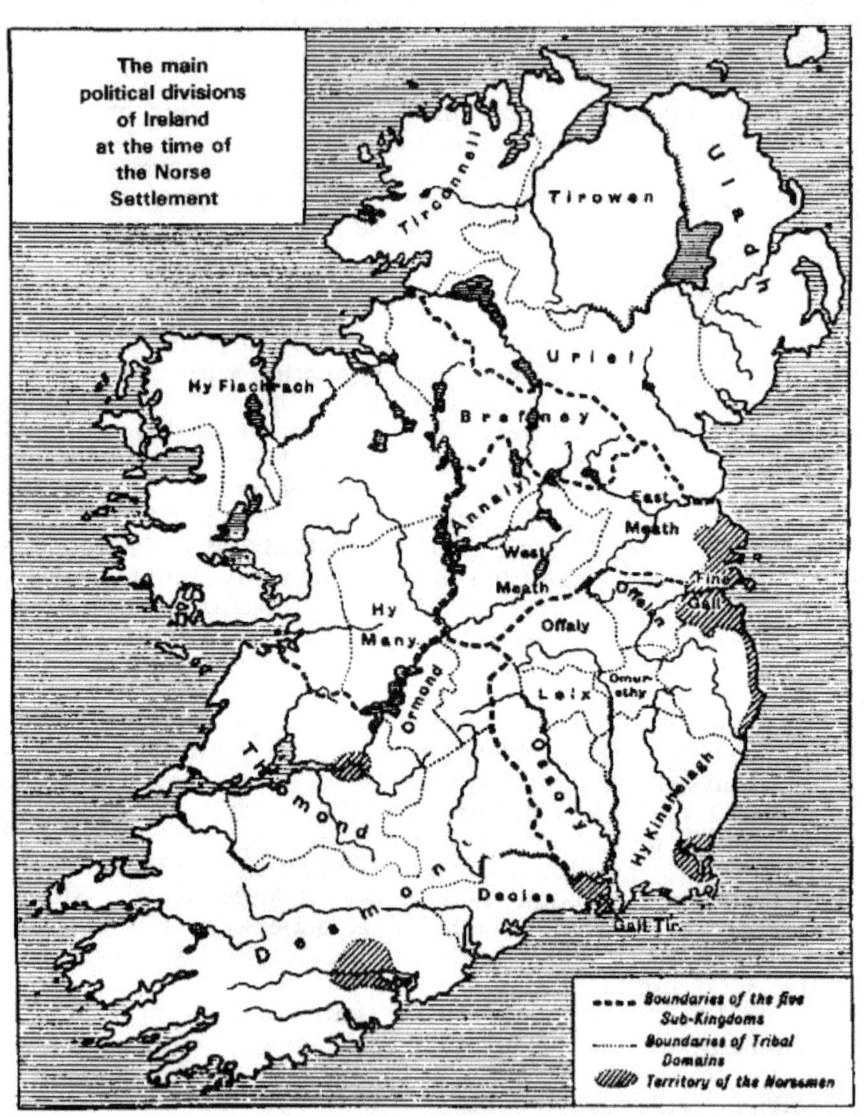

The main
political divisions
of Ireland
at the time of
the Norse
Settlement
Tirconnell
Tirowen
Uladh
Uriel
Hy Fiachrach
Brefney
Annaly
East
Meath
West
Meath
Hy
Many
Offelan
Fine
Gall
Offaly
Ormond
Leix
Omur
ethy
Ossory
Thomond
Hy Kinsellagh
Desmond
Decies
Gall Tir.
Boundaries of the five
Sub-Kingdoms
Boundaries of Tribal
Domains
Territory of the Norsemen

17

throne to his son, Con More. Henry died in 1489, after 60 years as a prominent leader and Chief in Ulster.

Con More, who now became Prince of Tyrone, was 120th on the pedigree. He was married to Elinor Fitzgerald, daughter of Thomas, the 7th Earl of Kildare. He had four sons - Art Og, John, Turlough and Con Baccah.

Con More, now Prince of Tyrone, had an act passed in 1401, which granted him the benefit of English law which was denied to his countrymen. Shortly after his installation, he was attacked by the O'Donnells, who were allied with the O'Neills of Clanaboy, who were always fueding with the chief of Tyrone, probably to shake off his overlordship. Con concluded an agreement with the O'Donnells over the tribute owed him for Innishowen. He invaded Louth and took hostages from the O'Kanes. He then built a house for the Franciscans at Dunganon.

In 1493, Con More, a brave and warlike man (brave and good, according to the annalists), was slain by his young brother Henry Og, who then assumed the Kingship of Tyrone. But Donal, his older brother was elected by the people. Donal was defeated and driven out by Henry Og. Later Donal reached an agreement with Henry Og and for large gifts of land, horses and armor and the release of his son, Hugh. He yielded the supremacy of Tyrone to Henry Og. In 1498, Henry Og invaded Tirconnell and in 1499, he was slain by the sons of Con More Tirlough and Con Bacach, in revenge for the murder of their father.

Donal then resumed the Lordship of Tyrone, but he was harried by his nephews. Donal died in 1509 and was succeeded by **Art of the Fews**, who was the Roydanna or Tanist, a very noble, intelligent man, who was succeeded in 1514 by Art Og, oldest son of Con More.

He was a distinguished captain. **Art Og**, after his installation as Prince of Tyrone, was opposed by the sons of Donal and the descendants of Art of Omagh, who he defeated, capturing their castles and a large quantity of military stores. He was then accepted as overlord by the McGuires, McMahons, O'Kanes, McGinnis and the Clanaboy O'Neills. After a short conflict, his brother, John, who was his Tanist, died in 1517. John was the ancestor of the Kinard branch of the O'Neills. Art Og died in 1519. From him are descended the clan Art Og O'Neills, Sliocht Art Ogs, etc. His sons were Niall Connalach, Henry Balbh, Cormac, Donal Tuathal and Rory.

Art Og was succeeded in the Lordship of Tyrone by his youngest brother, **Con Bacach**, a very controversial figure in Irish history, who in the beginning started to follow in the footsteps of his ancestors who were always ready to take up arms to drive the English invaders from their country and bring liberty and justice to their countrymen.

After several clashes with the English, **Con Bacach** and the Lord deputy signed a treaty with them, which they violated several times. Then Con O'Neill gathered his forces together after the deputy Grey laid waste and depopulated the countryside around Armagh and carried away with him an immense booty. Con O'Neill followed them into Meath, having with him, O'Donnell, McGuire, Magennnis, O'Kane, O'Hanlon and other allies. He laid waste to the English possessions from Atherdee in County Louth to Navan in Meath, but was surprised by the deputy and forced to retreat back to Ulster.

Then after another treaty was signed, he did for a time submit. Con then went to England, where he was persuaded to renouce the Title of O'Neill and Prince of Tyrone, receiving back from King Henry VIII the Anglo-Saxon title of Earl of Tyrone. His reputed son, **Matthew** received the title, Baron of Dunganon. Con Bacach and all the Irish chiefs renounced their Gaelic titles and received their land back with English titles.

The O'Neills and other chief families were for a long time prior to this event trying to hand their title and land down to their sons, which the Law of Tanistry prevented them from doing. In English Law, the title and lands go to the oldest son. The Prices of Tyrone from Owen More down were all making provisions for their sons. The majority of the Irish people were opposed to this transfer of all the lands to the chiefs as it did away with the democratic election of their leaders.

Shane O'Neill, called Shane the Proud, with other Ulster chiefs who resented the foreign title of Earl, rebelled against Con Bacach. Although Con was a good ruler and fought many battles again the English, driving them out of Ulster, this act alienated his subjects and his son, Shane, who was his Tanist, was elected the O'Neill in his place.

Con Bacach was married to Alice, daughter of Gerald Fitzgerald, 8th Earl of Kildare. He had issue by her - Shane, Tirlough, Felem and Mary. His other son, Matthew was born by another woman. Under the Brehon Law, children by concubines are legitimate if their father accepts them.

When Henry VIII of England conferred the Earldom of Tyrone on Con Bacach O'Neill, it was for life, with the remainder to his reputed son, Matthew and his heirs forever.

Matthew was a good soldier and Con was willing to have him for a successor. The King then gave him the title Baron of Dunganon. Now **Shane Con's** eldest legitimate son was opposed to this. Being an ambitious young man, he had himself designated the Tanist by a large portion of the clan. Under Irish law the Tanist was the successor to the chief. Shane, who now became the peoples' choice, forced his father to yield. Shane claimed and rightly so, that by Celtic law and usage, Con had no power to transfer the property of the Clan in which he had only a life interest and that the patent of Earl was null and void. Shane now drove his father and stepmother out of Ulster into the English pale.

Con Bacach died in 1557. His son, **Shane O'Neill** called Shane the Proud, was elected Prince of Tyrone. Shane was indignant to see his house degraded by his father taking the English title of Earl in place of the hereditary Prince of Tyrone and the illustrious title of O'Neill. Shane claimed he ruled by ancient right over the counties of McGinnis, McMahon, McGuire, O'Kane, O'Hanlon, McArtin, Duffirn, the Savages of Ards and had ancient rights over O'Rielly County, Clanaboy and the Route should belong to him and rent out the lands of small reputation and the Black Rent from the pale that was paid to his ancestors.

Queen Elizabeth of England acknowledged Shane as Chief of Tyrone, Derry and a large part of Antrim, but to the Irish he was King of Ulster from Dundalk to the river Erne. Shane was now continually in arms, either against the O'Donnells or his rival, his reputed half-brother, Matthew, the Baron of Dungannon, who was supported by the English. But Matthew was killed early in the war. The English then made Matthew's son, Brian Baron of Dungannon. The Queen then ordered the Lord Deputy to proceed to Ulster and establish Brian in Shane's place. Queen Elizabeth was, at that time, preparing to force the Protestant religion on the Irish people. The government imprisoned several bishops who refused to go along with the project.

Shane O'Neill, the most powerful and bravest Irish nobleman in the country, espoused the cause of the imprisoned Catholic Bishops and led his army in their support into the English pale with great success. After the campaign, Shane returned to Ulster to spend the Winter months there. During that time, he built a castle on the shores of Lough Neagh which he called Foonegal or hate of the Englishmen.

Hearing that Catherine McLean, wife of O'Donnell had landed in Donegal with 2,000 Scots, Shane swooped down on Donegal, capturing Calvough O'Donnell and his wife, carrying them prisoners into Tyrone. Catherine, who was previously married to the Earl of Argile, became Shane's paramour and had one son by Shane while she was his prisoner. Shane married her after her husband died. Their son was known in history as **Hugh Gravelock**. Catherine was and educated woman who could speak several languages. The Earl of Sussex, the Lord Lieutenant, gathered an army and march north to Armagh which he fortified. After some battles with Shane in which his army was always defeated with loss, Sussex became demoralized and withdrew his forces from Ulster and Shane resumed control of Ulster from Drogheda to the Erne. The Earl of Kildare, a relative of Shane, persuaded him to submit and go to London and meet the Queen face-to-face. Receiving a guarantee of safety, Shane left for England the 6th of January, 1562 attended by a company of his Gallowglasses, covered with coats of mail and armed with battleaxes. He was received by the Queen with her court and foreign ambasadors where Shane, the great O'Neill, cousin of St. Patrick and friend of the Queen, stated the injuries that goaded him into hostilities.

The Queen received him with great courtesy, but deferred her answers until the Baron of Dungannon should arrive in London. Shane, becoming alarmed at this delay, prepared to go home immediately, relying on the protection promised him, but was given to understand that the promise was carefully worded and mentioned no date for his return. Shane then wrote to the Queen and her ministers and his close relations with the Spanish Ambassador.

In April, when word was received that the 2nd Baron of Dungannon was slain, Shane was permitted to leave. Before Shane O'Neill was allowed to leave England, he was forced to sign an agreement, under duress, acknowledging the Queen as his soverign and giving up his claim to the Kingship of Ulster, but leaving him in supreme authority over Tyrone.

During the time Shane was in England, he made many friends who remained his friends for a long time afterward. Shane, a widower during this time, was said to be looking for an English wife. Frances Ratcliff, sister of the Earl of Sussex was his choice. Shane was also supposed to be aspiring for the hand of Elizabeth, the Queen. A Protestant, one Adam Loftus, a native of Yorkshire was appointed Archbishop of Armagh by Queen Elizabeth and soon began to write to the Lord Lieutenant Sussex with suspicions about Shane which gained ground and Sussex again marched his troops north against Shane, who was then forced to take up arms.

Shane met the English army near Dundalk on April 13, 1563. In a skirmish, Sussex managed to cross the Blackwater, but on April 16th, fearing a surprise, he retired to Dundalk. In the beginning of June he advanced to Dungannon, but was forced to retreat by Shane. A peace was then concluded between Shane and Sussex.

Shane then renewed his suit for Frances Ratcliff. During the negotiations, John Smith, a creature of Sussex, tried to kill Shane with a gift of poisoned wine which almost succeeded. The Queen expressed indignation at the detestable attempt. Shane then declared war on the McDonnells of Antrim who rejected his claims of supremacy and his overtures for an alliance.

Shane marched his army into Antrim, capturing several of McDonnells' castles. Then, after a battle at Glentow, the Scots were defeated and 700 of them slain. Shane captured their Chief, James McDonnell and wounded James McDonnell's brother, Sorley Boy and 19 other Scotish chiefs. He then banished the Scots out of the Glens of Antrim.

The Queen, growing alarmed at the growing strength of Shane, sent over Sidney to Ireland as a deputy, who wrote to Shane requesting and interview with him at Dundalk, which he declined, stating that, by the Articles of 1563, he was absolved from any obligation to wait upon the Viceroy and beside, his life had been threatened by poison and dagger, that he was once unlawfully detained and had to give 19 of his best pledges before he obtained his liberty.

However, he agreed to meet Stokely and Dowdel, whom he received kindly. At a banquet in their honor, he told them he would not accept the title of Earl unless it was something better and higher as he was by blood and power better than the best of them. He agreed that the Queen was his sovereign. He never asked for peace but at her seeking. Shane said that when he was in England he was held until he signed things that were against his honor and could not perform. He told them that he could bring into the field 1,000 horse and 4,000 foot soldiers, that he could march to the walls of Dublin and back without a fight; that his ancestors were Kings of Ulster; that Ulster was his and should be. That Bagnel would never come into Newry or Kildare into Dundrum and Lecale. By the sword he had won them and by the sword he would keep them.

In 1566, he had gained possession of all Ulster and McGuire and Calough O'Donnell took refuge in Dublin. He then went into Connacht, receiving tribute from all the principal chiefs in recognition of his sovereignty, except the Anglo-Norman Earl of Clanrickard, from whom he took 4,000 cattle back to Tyrone. He fortified Lifford in the north and Dundrum and Lecale and threatened Dundalk. He wrote Charles IX of Lorraine, offering him allegiance if he would send 5,000 men to his aid.

In July, he entered the pale and beseiged Dundalk. During that time the English sent 1,000 men under Col Randolp into Derry where they built a fort. Shane beseigned them with 2,500 men and 300 horse, but was repulsed. In the fight Col Randolp was killed. Shortly after, the magazines exploded, demolishing the fort and killing 700 soldiers. The rest escaped back to Dublin. Shane next defeated the English army invading Tyrone at the battle of Red Sagums, killing 400 of them. Shane then went into Donegal, Fermanagh and Connacht.

Calvough O'Donnell, dying suddenly, his brother, Hugh was elected in his place. This Hugh, who was befriended by Shane, did, with the help of the English, invade Tyrone, wasting, destorying and driving off cattle. He also burned Strabane. Shane gathered his army to retaliate. Shane and his army reached the shores of Lough Swilly and began crossing at the fords while the tide was out. He was attacked by O'Donnell and the English army, who, with the help of the incoming tide, defeated Shane's army with a loss of more than 2,000 men.

Unable to get an army together again and deserted by many of his most trusted followers, including Hugh O'Neill of the Fews, McGuire, McGrath and McArdle, the President of his council, perhaps all bribed with English money.

Shane was then forced to make overtures to the McDonnells of Antrim, who agreed to help. Relying on their promise, he went to their camp in Cushendun with a small escort and was received with apparent goodwill. During the banquet that followed in Shane's honor, the Scots provoked an argument, which led to a quarrel in which Shane was killed with his few followers. The Scots cut off his head and sent it to Dublin, where it was spiked on the castle walls.

Shane was only 37 years old when he was killed. And thus died Shane O'Neill, a man who sacrificed everything for his country. Had his example been followed by the rest of his countrymen, Ireland might never have been reduced.

As for the rest of the nobles, some of them took English titles which bound them to the government, thereby becoming subjects.

In order to reduce Shane O'Neill, Queen Elizabeth spent a huge sum of money, with the loss of 3,500 English soldiers killed, a large loss in those days. After Shane's death, his estates were confiscated for the Queen's use by an act of Parliament. It included Tyrone, Derry, Clandeboy, the Fews, Antrim, the greater part of Down, Armagh and Monaghan.

Shane's sons were children when he died and were unable to succeed him so that Shane's dynasty died with him. In later years some of his sons contested the Chieftanship of Tyrone, to no avail. **Tirlough Lynough** O'Neill, Shane's cousin and Tanist, was made Chief of Tyrone with the Queen's consent. This Tirlough was the grandson of Art Og O'Neill, who was King of Ulster from 1515 to 1519 A.D.

When **Tirlough Lynough** O'Neill was elected Chief of Tyrone with Queen Elizabeth's consent, which to gain, he had to renounce all claims to paramountcy over the border lords outside Tyrone. He also agree to leave Hugh O'Neill Baron of Dungannon, in full possession of his private estates.

Hugh O'Neill was educated in England and was supported by the government as Chief of Tyrone, which incensed Tirlough Lynough O'Neill so much that he rejected his English allegiance and declared himself hereditary Prince of Ulster. To protect himself from English wrath, he married Agnes Campbell, widow of James McDonnell, who was able to supply him with plenty of Scotch mercenaries. That, and an alliance with Sorley Boy McDonnell, who had landed in Antrim with 4,000 Scots, prevented the English from overrunning Ulster. They were married on Rathlin Island off the coast of northeast Ulster, near the Giants Causeway.

Tirlough's usual home was at Strabane. He had other castles at Toome and Castle Roe. The English, unable to make any headway in Ulster, proposed a treaty which was ratified by Tirlough who was not a strong man like Shane O'Neill. The English then began to weaken his power, so much so, that he was forced to divide Tyrone with Hugh O'Neill, the Baron of Dungannon; Tirlough taking the northern half and the baron taking the southern half.

In 1572, Tirlough, allied with O'Donnell and Brian McPhalem O'Neill, appeared at the Leinster border with 4,000 men to prevent the English from planting Ulster. But a peace was concluded in 1574.

In 1583, Tirlough and the Baron of Dungannon were in Dublin and in 1585, the Dublin Parliament created Hugh O'Neill Earl of Tyrone, in preparation to make him Chief of all of Tyrone.

The sons of Shane O'Neill, called the McSeans, were now making a bid for the Chieftainship and were supported by Tirlough Lynough. They were opposed to Earl Hugh O'Neill who was then supported by the English. The Earl took one of them, called Hugh of the Fetters, prisoner and hung him.

In 1588, Tirlough Lynough O'Neill consented to allow Hugh O'Neill to be inaugurated the O'Neill in the Rath of Tullaghoge. Tirlough Lynough O'Neill died in 1595 and was buried at Ardstraw in Strabane. Tirlough Lynough had three sons - Sir Arthur, Henry and Cormac.

On the death of Tirlough Lynough O'Neill, **Hugh O'Neill,** the third **Baron of Dungannon** and second Earl of Tyrone, became **Prince of Tyrone.** When Hugh was nine years old, he was taken **by Sir Henry** Sidney to England. He was educated at **Penthurst in Ken and in London.** His patrons brought him up in the new religion. While still a young man, he was for a time in the court of Elizabeth where he became a favorite and was highly honored. Returning to Ireland in 1568, he was appalled by the English destructive policy there of plunder and robbery and for a time he remained loyal and led a troop of horse for the English during the Desmond rebellion in 1569.

Hugh now began to build up his resources, allowed by the government to keep 200 soldiers in his pay, which he rotated after training them in the new firearms. In 1588, he gave aid and comfort to the survivors of Spanish Armada ships wrecked on the coast of Innishowen, which made the English suspicious of his loyalty.

In 1590, he was involved in the hanging of Hugh Gravloch, son of Shane O'Neill. After a trip to London, he received pardon from the Queen.

Hugh O'Neill divorced his first wife in 1574 and his second wife died in 1591. In the same year he eloped with Mapel Bagenal, a daughter of Marshal Bagenal, an English miitary commander. Also in 1591, he helped Red Hugh O'Donnell escape from Dublin Castle. In 1595, on the death of Tirlough Lynough, Hugh O'Neill renounced the title of Earl and declared himself an independent Prince. In the same year he was proclaimed a traitor to the Crown.

His wife Mapel died at Dungannon in the Spring of 1596 and shortly after he married his fourth wife, Catherine MaGinnis. Also, in 1595, he defeated Sir John Norris at the battle of Clontibert with a loss to the English of 600 dead. After several more battles with the English, in one of which Sir John Norris was mortally wounded, a peace was arranged in 1596.

A new Deputy Lord Brough was sent to Ireland in 1597. In August, 1598, he ordered Marshal Bagenal to Ulster with 5,000 soldiers. He was met at the Yellow Ford on the Blackwater by O'Neill. In the battle Bagenal was slain with 24 of his chief officers and up to 3,000 of his men. The battle of the Yellow Ford was a disaster for the English. Beside their loses in manpower, they lost all their baggage, artillery and instruments of war, thirty-four stands of colors, stores of arms and 12,00 pieces of gold. The Irish lost 200 killed and 600 wounded. This great victory of O'Neill raised the hopes of other Irish Chieftains who had submitted to the English, who began to speak of O'Neill as Prince of Ireland. He did indeed take his army through Leinster into Munster where he conferred with the leading noblemen of those provinces.

Queen Elizabeth, becoming alarmed, sent her favorite, the Earl of Essex to Ireland in 1599 with royal powers and 20,000 men. After a disastrous march through Leinster and Munster, he met O'Neill near Dundalk in September, 1599 and a truce until May 1st, 1600 was agreed on.

Essex returned to England and was imprisoned in the Tower of London and later executed for treason. The Queen then sent a monster, Lord Mountjoy as the deputy and another monster, George Carew was made President of Munster. Mountjoy came to Ireland with one purpose—to defeat the Irish by starvation and began his operations by landing Sir Henry Dowcra at Lough Foyle where he built four forts to harass O'Neill and O'Donnell and prevent them from sending troops to Leinster and Munster. Dowcra had with him 4,000 troops. He was joined by Sir Arthur O'Neill, son of Tirlough Lynough, who became the Queen's O'Neill against Hugh.

Mountjoy marched into Ulster with an army and began destroying the crops. He was met by O'Neill, who defeated him in two battles, forcing him to return to Dublin. In September, 1601, a small Spanish force of 2,600 men landed at Kinsale where Mountjoy quickly beseiged them. O'Neill marched his army into Leinster to harass and draw Mountjoy away from Kinsale, which he would not leave. O'Neill and O'Donnell arrived at Kinsale in December, 1601. Their combined force of 6,000 men confronted Mountjoy, who had 16,000 men. O'Neill advised caution, but was overruled by O'Donnell and Del Aguila. They decided to attack on December 24th, 1601. But through confusion and the Spaniard failing to sally out as arranged, the battle ended in defeat for the Irish.

The battle of Kinsale marked the end of the Gaelic system in Ireland. O'Neill returned to Ulster to be harassed by Dowcra, but held out for two years until March, 1603 when he accepted terms and surrendered to Mountjoy at Mellifort, County Louth.

When O'Neill learned in April that he was tricked (the Queen had died before his surrender), he wept with rage. He then went to England to meet the new King, James I, who gave him his lands and title back, promising him full religious freedom.

Long before the war was ended, many of the Irish chiefs had deserted the cause and joined Mountjoy and some of them were with him at Kinsale. Before Hugh O'Neill's surrender to Mountjoy, he was deserted by the most prominent O'Neill families, including his own half-brother, Henry O'Neill, Chief of the Fews in Armagh; the Art Og O'Neills, the branch Sir Arthur O'Neill belong to; the Kinard O'Neills; the Clanaboy O'Neills; his son-in-law, Donald O'Kane, Chief of Keenaght. When Hugh O'Neill returned from England with the King's pardon in his pocket, he had hopes of being left alone. But the Dublin government baited him and took from him great tracks of land and instigated plots to involve him and Rory O'Donnell. They began to charge him with conspiracy and treason and summoned him to Dublin before the council, where he, with O'Donnell appeared but no decision was reached. They were ordered to appear again and were forbidden to practice their religion. He heard from friendly sources that he and Rory O'Donnell would be arrested and tried for treason, perhaps executed. In despair, they decided to flee to Europe (the famous flight of the Earls).

At midnight on the 14th of September, 1607, the Earls left Ireland, never to return. Earl Hugh O'Neill and his countess, Catherana; their sons, Hugh, John and Bernard; his nephews, Art Og, Owen Roe, Hugh Og and Fadrocha and many of his clansmen. With O'Donnell were Caffar, his brother; Nuala, his sister, wife of Nial Garve, the traitor; Hugh, the Earl's son, one year old and many of his retainers. In Europe, they were received as heros. O'Neill at that time was called the best General in Europe. Then on to Rome, where they received a pension from the Pope. O'Neill died on July 20th, 1616 and was buried with great pomp at San Pietro in Rome beside his son.

The flight of the Earls gave the Dublin government the excuse they were looking for, the attainder of the Earls for treason with their adherents and the escheatment of their property. This opened the Ulster Counties for planting, giving the English thieves in Dublin the opportunity to plunder the native Irish of all their lands, without any compensation.

The planting of Ulster by the English and Scotch was one of the greatest acts of thievery that was ever carried out by any government up until that time. It created centuries of ill-will and bloodshed down to the present time. The native population, with the exception of a few O'Neill families who joined the English before the war was over. All others lost their lands which were bestowed on English and Scotch Protestants who hung the Irish like dogs.

The escheated counties were divided in lots of 1,000, 1,500 and 2,000 acres which were known as small, middle and larger proportions. Those proportions were assigned to various English and Scotch undertakers by lot. Others were assigned to servitors and native Irish chiefs. The first distribution was made to 168 undertakers, 41 servitors and 63 natives. Many of the natives in a short time were swindled out of their allotment. Any of the natives that owned land before the 1641 rebellion were all transplanted to Connacht.

The undertakers and servitors were allowed two years before they had to pay rent, while the natives had to start paying in the first year. Those O'Neills that received land during the plantation were: Sir Henry O'Neill of the Fews, half-brother to

Earl Hugh, got 9,000 acres; Cormac McBaron, Tyrone's brother, got 2,000 acres; Henry and Con, sons of Shane O'Neill, got 1,500 acres each; Henry Og of the Kinard O'Neills, received 5,000 acres; Tirlough O'Neill of the McArt Og, grandson of Tirlough Lynough O'Neill, got 3,500 acres; Art McBaron, another brother of Earl Hugh, got 2,000 acres; Brian Crossagh, son of Cormac Mc Baron, received 1,000 acres and a few other O'Neills received a few acres each.

The O'Neills

The **O'Neill's of Tyrone** coronation ceremoney was conducted with all the pomp and splendor of the old Gaelic world at the Tullaghoge fort in the Parish of Desertcreight, nine miles north of Dungannon, on the way to Cookstown where a large stone sitting in an open field served as the coronation chair. The O'Neills were installed by the Chief of the O'Hagans, hereditary justiciars of Tyrone. O'Hagan installed the O'Neill by putting on O'Neill's foot a golden slipper or sandal and that's the reason for the sandal in the O'Hagan Coast of Arms.

Hugh O'Neill, the great Earl of Tyrone was the last O'Neill to be enthroned there. After he surrendered in 1602, Mountjoy, the Lord Deputy had it broken up to symbolize the end of the rule of the O'Neills in Tyrone.

The **Clanaboy O'Neills** had their own installation on the Hill of Castlereagh, about two miles outside Belfast, also on a stone chair. Their last Chief to be installed there was Con O'Neill in the reign of James I. The last lineal representative in Ireland of the Clanaboy O'Neills was John Bruce Richard O'Neill, third viscount and Baron O'Neill of Shane's Castle, County Antrim. He died in February, 1855. His estates then went to the Rev. William Chichester, a great grandson of Mary O'Neill, heiress of French John O'Neill, who then took the name of O'Neill and was created Baron O'Neill of Shane's Castle. From that family descends the Lords Rathcavan and the Baronets of Cleegan, also former Captain O'Neill Terence O'Neill, prime minister of the six counties. They are all really Chichester in the male line.

The Bansheee of the O'Neills of Ulster

According to old Irish legends, some of Ireland's great families had Banshee's who warned them of deaths in the family. The O'Neills had one call Mauveen. Mauveen of The O'Neills was sometimes seen in the form of a very old woman with long white hair falling to her shoulders and dressed in ghostly white clothes. In the stillness of the night before an O'Neill died, she would give one or two blood curdling and mournful cries while floating around the stricken house.

THE CORONATION CEREMONY

of the
Tyrone O'Neills
By
Thomas Davis
The Inspired Young Irish Poet

Come, look on the pomp when they 'make an O'Neill';
The muster of dynasts — O'Hagan, O'Sheil
O'Kane and O'Hanlon, O'Breslin and all.
From gentle Aird-Uladth to wild Donegal;
St. Patrick's comharba (successor), with bishops thirteen,
And ollavs and brehons and minstrels are seen
Round Tulach'og rath, like the bees in the spring
All swarming to honour a true Irish king!

And he must have come from a conquering race—
The heir of their valour, their glory, their grace;
His frame must be stately, his step must be fleet,
His body be trained to each warrior-feat;
His face, as the harvest moon, steadfast and clear,
A head to enlighten, a spirit to cheer;
While the foremost to rush where the battle-brands ring,
And the last to retreat is a true Irish king!

Yet not for his courage, his strength, or his name,
Can he from the clansmen their fealty claim.
The poorest, the highest, choose freely today
The chief that tonight they'll as truly obey;
For loyalty springs from a people's consent,
And the knee that is forced had been better unbent—
The Sassenach serfs no such homage can bring
As the Irishman's choice of a true Irish king!

Unsandalled he stands on on the foot-dented rock,
Like a pillar-stone fixed against ever shock.
Round, round is the rath on a far-seeing hill,
Like his blemishless honour and vigilant will.
The grey-beards are telling how chiefs by the score

Have been crowned on the "Rath of Kings' heretofore;
While crowded, yet ordered, within its green ring.
Are the dynasts and priests round the true Irish king.

The chronicler read him the laws of the clan
And pledged him to bide by their blessing and ban;
His scian and his sword are unbluckled to show
They they only were meant for a foreigner foe;
A white willow wand has been put in his hand—
A type of pure, upright, and gentle command—
While hierarchs are blessing, the slipper they fling,
And O'Kane then proclaims him a true Irish king!

Thrice looked he to heaven with thanks and with prayer,
Thrice looked to his borders with sentinel stare—
To the waves of Lough Neagh, to the heights of Strabane—
And thrice on his allies and thrice on his clan;
One clash on their bucklers!—one more!—they are still;
What means the deep pause on the crest of the hill?
Why gaze they above him? a war-eagle's wing!
'Tis an omen! Hurrah! for the true Irish king."

The story is told that when Shane O'Neill, of Tyrone, was approached by an emissary of Elizabeth and informed that she had the great scion of the House and created him "Earl of Tyrone"—Niall cried out: "Earl, me?, no earls — I am THE O'NEILL."

One of the Irish poets has immortalized this episode in the following verses:

"I scorn your Lady's honors—I scorn her titles vain,
A Prince am I of high degree and of a fair domain;
Peace have I never craved from her, but ever she from me,
I am a king in kingly right, and hold my kingdom free.

Heremon's blood is in my veins—I feel it swelling high,
And Eoghan's of the iron arm, and of the flashing eye;
Their forms are melted into dust—their spirit is not gone,
I owe no fealty to your Queen, and I will yield her none.

She boasts her ancient Norman line, but tell me, can she trace
A pedigree as long and proud as of my noble race?
And can she dream that I would stand among her modern peers,
I, whose sides were Princes for twice a thousand years?

What, though indeed at last arose a traiter to his line,

(Alas the day!—that I should name the recreant sire of mine)
My trusty glaive has gained again the rights of Cinel-Eoghain,
And by its flash will I remain my kindom of Tyrone.

Go, tell her, though MacCarty Mor has bent him like a churl,
And risen from beneath her hand, a belted English Earl;
That Shane the Proud is prouder far, and not for England's
    Crown
Would he exchange the name O'NEILL, or lay its honors down.

Say that ye found him all prepared for peace, or for the fray,
Standing upon his native hill, as stern, as free as they;
And that, were all the rest her slaves, there would he stand
    ALONE—
Defying from his rocky crest, the foemen of Tyrone."

The O'Neill's of Tyrone

According to the Laws of Tanistry, all the members of the house of O'Neill were eligible to become King of Ireland, as well as to any of the principalities belonging to the family. They all had the right to be styled heirs to the throne of Ireland and of Ulster, hereditary Prince of Tyrone or of Clanaboy, as the case may be.

For some time before the Tyrone wars, the O'Neill family had divided into the O'Neill's of Tyrone, the O'Neill's of Clanaboy and the O'Neill's of the Fews. The Princes of Tyrone ruled over the present counties of Tyrone, Derry, Innishowen, in Donegal, parts of Armagh and the adjoining counties. The second Lordship Canaboy was divided into North and South; the former between the rivers Ravel and Lagan. It was composed of the modern Baronies of the two Antrims, the two Toomes, two Belfast, lower Massarene and Carrickfergus; south of the River Lagan, the two Baronies of Upper and Lower Castlereagh.

The third Lorship, the Fews, was composed of the Baronies of Upper and Lower Fews in Armagh. By the 16th century, the Tyrone O'Neill's had splintered into several families, often fueding with each other, one or more of them always in opposition to the ruling family and generally supported by the English, whose policy was to divide and conquer. So that in all the conflicts with the English, you would find a Queen's or King's O'Neill, as the case may be, fighting on their side.

This policy was used by the English government in Ireland to destroy all the great Gaelic families in the country. Shane the Proud and Tirlough Lynough O'Neill had the Dungannon O'Neill's in opposition when Earl Hugh O'Neill of the Dungannon house became Prince of Tyrone. He was opposed by the sons of Shane O'Neill, the Clan Art Og and later by the Kinard O'Neill's and also by the O'Neill's of the Fews. When Earl Hugh went down, they all fell with him. Never trust the English is a good policy.

The O'Neill's of Dungannon

This family began with Matthew, the reputed oldest son of Con Bacach O'Neill, who was created Earl of Tyrone by Henry VIII of England. Henry also created Matthew Baron of Dungannon, with his right to the succession of the Earldom. Matthew was ousted by his half-brother, Shane the Proud and finally killed in a skirmish with some of Shane's followers.

Matthew was married and had at least four sons - Brian, Hugh, Cormac and Art. Brian, on his father's death, became Baron of Dungannon, but was killed by Tirlough Lynough O'Neill, who was then Shane's Tanist. Then Hugh, Matthew's second son, became Baron of Dungannon and later the great Earl of Tyrone. Hugh O'Neill was married four times and had five sons and four daughters. Hugh, his eldest son, Baron of Dungannon, was engaged to be married to the Earl of Argile's daughter, but it fell through. He fled with his father to Europe and died in Rome without issue. He was 25 years old.

Tyrone's second son, Henry, was sent to Spain to be educated as a soldier, he was promoted to Colonel of the Irish regiment in service for Spain in 1605. He was in high favor with the King of Spain and remained Colonel of the Irish regiment until his death in 1626. He became Earl of Tyrone on his father's death in 1616. He left no issue.

John Tyrone's third son succeeded to the title and to the command of the Irish regiment, held by his brother. He was also highly honored by King Philip IV, who gave him the rank of Major-General in the army. He also had great influence with the Court of Rome. He would have gone to Ireland in 1641 if he was not obliged to go to Catalonia, where he fell fighting the insurgents. He also died without issue.

Brian, the fourth son of Tyrone, was found hung in his apartment in Brussels with his hand tied behind his back. He was a page to the Archduke of Austria, who was Governor of the Netherlands for Spain.

Tyrone's fifth son, Con, was left behind with his foster-father when the Earls fled to Europe. He was captured, brought up a Protestant by Sir Toby Cawfield and lived out his life in Ireland. All Tyrone's sons died without issue.

The O'Neill's of Dungannon
(Brothers of Earl Hugh)

Brian, the second Baron of Dungannon, Earl Hugh's elder brother, was killed early in his life in a skirmish with Tirlough Lynough O'Neill during the time Shane O'Neill was in England. Brian was supported by the English, who were endeavoring to oust Shane O'Neill.

Sir Cormac McBaron O'Neill, Earl Hugh's next brother, was a good soldier who commanded at the seige of Portmore 60 horse and 300 foot. He was in command of 600 foot in the Earl's army during the later stages of the war. Sir Cormac reported the flight of the Earls to the government. He was then arrested and confined in the Tower of London, where he died. Sir Cormac had two sons. One, Brian Crossagh O'Neill received 1000 acres at the plantation of Ulster. He was executed by the English in 1616 for a supposed plot to murder the planters and free the Earl's son, Con, held by Sir Toby Caufield.

Sir Cormac's other son, Con McCormac O'Neill, after service in the Spanish army, where he was a Captain, returned to Ireland in 1642, where he was made a colonel in the Irish army and later at Lt.-General to his cousin, Owen Roe O'Neill, but was laid aside due to some discontent. He surrendered with other Ulster leaders, in 1652 and was allowed to go to Europe and received a license to transport 1000 men from Drogheda for service in the Spanish army. He was supposed to have married a niece of the Duchess of Artoss.

Earl Hugh's other brother, Art McBaron, served in the Tyrone wars. He received 2000 acres at the plantation of Ulster. His oldest son, Brian McArt was killed during the Tyrone wars. His other sons were Art Og, the father of Hugh Dubb O'Neill, the famous defender of Clonmel, County Tipperary against Cromwell and Owen Roe O'Neill, the commander of the Ulster Irish army during the 1641 war for freedom. He gave the English army a disastrous defeat at the battle of Benburb.

The O'Neill's of Dungannon
(Owen Roe O'Neill)

Owen Roe O'Neill, son of Art McBaron, a brother of Earl Hugh O'Neill of Tyrone, left Ireland with his uncle and studied in the Irish College of Salamanca in Spain. From there he was appointed to a sergeantcy of Halberdiers, the foot guards to the Spanish monarchs.

In 1625, Owen was transferred to the Spanish Netherlands, from a list of the Irish abroad who might be dangerous to the English. Owen Roe was listed as a Major of the Irish regiment in the Netherlands, where he won the high honors in the Spanish service. His gallant defense of Arris in 1640 against three French Marshals won for him the aclaim of all Europe.

When his countrymen called, Owen Roe left rank and station abroad to aid them in their struggle for freedom. In 40 battles with the English, Owen Roe only lost one. He landed in 1642 at Castle Doe on the coast of Donegal and was given the command of the small Ulster army, which was untrained. At the battle of Benburb in May, 1646, Owen Roe had 5,000 men against an English army of almost 7,000 men under General Monro. In that battle the English were defeated with a loss of 3,500 men and all their equipment, the most disastrous defeat they ever suffered in Ireland.

In 1649, Owen Roe had 5,000 foot and 500 horse and was preparing to march against Cromwell when he died on November 6th, 1649 at Lough Oughter Castle. His death was attributed to a pair of poisoned riding boots, given him by Colonel Plunket while in Derry.

Owen Roe was one of Ireland's greatest patriots, a truly remarkable man whose life had never been sullied by any mean or dishonorable act. Owen Roe was married to Rose O'Doherty and had five sons - Henry, who was hung by Coote after the battle of Scarriffhollis. He was married and had a son Hugh. Brian, the second son was married and had a son, Owen, the last Earl of Tyrone in exile. Owen Roe's other sons were Con, John and Lewis. All lived in Europe.

The O'Neill's of Dungannon
(Hugh Dubb O'Neill)

Major-General Hugh Dubb O'Neill was a son of Art Og, a younger brother of Owen Roe O'Neill and grandson of Art McBaron, a brother of Earl Hugh O'Neil. Hugh Dubb was born in the Spanish Netherlands where his father was an officer in the army of the Archduke.

Two sons of Art McBaron were listed in the English state papers of 1608 as Captain Art Og O'Neill (father of Major Hugh Dubb) and Captain Owen Roe O'Neill (General Owen Roe). Hugh Dubb received his military training in the Spanish army. Hugh Dubb returned to Ireland with his uncle, Owen Roe. He was Lt.-Colonel at the battle of Clones in 1643, where he was captured and remained a prisoner of the English until 1646, after the battle of Benburb, when he was exchanged for English prisoners.

During the illness of Owen Roe, he was in command of a section of the Ulster Army. He was dispatched with Lt.-General

Farrell and 2,000 men to assist the Earl of Ormonde in Munster and undertook the task of defending Clonmel with 1,200 men. Hugh Dubb's defense of Clonmel, against a vastly superior English army of 8,000, commanded by Cromwell himself, made him one of the most distinguished soldiers of his day.

After driving Cromwell's army out of Clonmel twice with huge English losses, Hugh Dubb was forced, through lack of ammunition, to leave the town at night and conveyed his small force to Waterford, where he was refused admittance by the governor, Preston. He then marched to Limerick where he was made Governor. He defended the city against the forces of Ireton, Cromwell's successor, until the city was betrayed by Major Fennell in October, 1651.

Exempt from pardon, O'Neill was sentenced to death. In January, 1652, he was sent to London and lodged in the Tower. The intervention of the Spanish Ambassador in London saved him from death and he was allowed to go to the Continent and was given permission to transport Irish soldiers to Spain.

In 1660, after the death of the last of Earl Hugh's sons, Hugh Dubb assumed the title Earl of Tyrone. Hugh Dubb died in Spain. He bequeathed the Earldom of Tyrone to Hugh, son of Henry, son of Owen Roe.

Sons of Shane O'Neill, The Proud

Henry O'Neill is shown in some genealogies as the oldest son of Shane, the Proud. In others, he is shown as the third or fourth. Shane O'Neill had seven sons — Sean Og, Con, Tirlough, Henry, Art, Hugh, Brian Henry, who was a political prisoner for most of his early adult life.

He was held as a pledge by Queen Elizabeth for most of his early youth. In September, 1581, Henry escaped from Sir Henry Sidney into Tyrone where he became a leader in opposition to Tirlough Lynough O'Neill, who was at that time Prince of Tyrone. He was captured by Tirlough Lynough in 1584 and turned over to the English who confined him as a prisoner in Dublin Castle. Henry escaped from there on Christmas, 1593 with his brother Art and Hugh Roe O'Donnell.

He didn't go to Glenmalure with O'Donnell and Art, but made his way up to the north. He then opposed Hugh, Earl of Tyrone for the Chieftanship of the O'Neill's. Henry was captured by the Earl of Tyrone in 1584 and held a prisoner in a Cronnoge Island until the Earl submitted in 1602, when he was released with his brothers, Con and Brian.

Henry received 1500 acres of land at the plantation of Ulster in the Barony of Oirer in Armagh, called Camlough.

After his death it was seized by Sir Toby Caulfield, the usual procedure used by the English planters to steal the land from the natives. Henry was married and had at least one son, Phalem, who served some time with the Irish regiment in Flanders, returning to Ireland after a disagreement with the colonel, who was the son of Earl Hugh of Tyrone.

Phalem then applied for admission to Lord Conway's regiment of horse. This Phalem is often confused with Sir Phalem O'Neill, the leader of the 1641 rebellion against the English in Ulster.

GENEALOGY

Shane O'Neill	Catherine McDonnell	Catherine McClean	Mary McGuire
Henry Daughter Phalem	Hugh, Art, Sean Og		Con, Brian, Tirlough, Neil

The Sons of Shane, The Proud

Con McShane O'Neill, the eldest son of Shane O'Neill by his third wife, a daughter of Sean Og McGuire, Con is first heard of in 1584 when he was released by Tirlough Lynough O'Neill who succeeded his father as Prince of Tyrone, who had held him for three years. It was reported that Tirlough had actually disowned his own son, Sir Arthur O'Neill of Newtown and adopted Con instead.

Tirlough Lynough also committed his own safety to Con, who was at that time opposed to the Earl of Tyrone. Tirlough Lynough continued to support Con until the end of 1590. In May of that year, Con was in Dublin under the protection of the Lord Deputy, where he alleged that Tyrone had tried to get McGuire to murder him. In November of 1590, Tirlough Lynough composed his difference with Hugh O'Neill, Earl of Tyrone which did not include Con or his brothers.

From 1595 to 1602, Con and his brothers were held prisoners by the Earl of Tyrone. At the plantation of Ulster, Con received 1,500 acres of land in the Barony of Coole, County Fermanagh, called Clabby, with 450 acres in Demense, where he built a bawn of sod with a strong stone house. He had three freeholders with 60 acres each.

When Con died in 1632, supposedly without heirs, his estate reverted to the Crown and was bestowed to John Conley, a Dublin merchant. Con O'Neill was married and had three sons,

Art Og, Sean and Hugh. His son, Art Og took part in the war of 1641. He was a captain of horse.

After the flight of the Earl of Tyrone, Con McShane assumed the Chieftanship of the O'Neills, which his descendants claimed until recent times, when they became extinct. His brother, **Sean Og McShane O'Neill** was killed by the O'Reilly's when he and Con invaded their territory in 1641.

Another brother, **Hugh Gravlagh**, Shane's son by Catherine MacLean, brought up in Scotland returned to Ireland and began harassing the Earl of Tyrone until he was captured by the McGuires and sold to the Earl, who had him condemned to death and hung.

Another son of Shane, the Proud, Brian, spent the early part of his life as a prisoner of Tirlough Lynough or of the Earl of Tyrone. At the plantation of Ulster, he moved to Clabby in Fermanagh with his brother, Con, perhaps as one of the freeholders. Brian was married and left issue.

The O'Neill's of Clan Art Og

This family of the O'Neill's were descended from Art Og O'Neill, eldest son of Con More O'Neill. Art Og was Prince of Tyrone from 1514 to 1519 A.D. Art had lands in the Barony of Strabane, Tyrone. The family owned Castle Derg and the Crannog of Lough Laeghrie near Lifford, described as a country 10 miles long, mostly bog and wood.

Art Og had six sons - Niall Connaleagh (1511 to 1545). He was Tanist to his uncle, Con Bacach; Henry, who died in 1526; Cormac who died in 1528; Donal, who died in 1522; Twihall, who died in 1538 and Brian, deceased in 1542.

Niall Connaleagh O'Neill, from being fostered by the Connaleachs, seems to have had bad relations with Con Bacach, Prince of Tyrone. At one time Niel was supported by the English for Tyrone Chief against Con Bacach. Niall had four sons -Tirlough Lynough, Con, Brian and Art Og.

Tirlough Lynough O'Neill was elected Prince of Tyrone after Shane O'Neill's death in 1565 and remained Prince of Tyrone for almost 40 years. Tirlough Lynough built a large army, many of them Scots brought over to him by his wife, Agnes Campbell. With their help, he was able to keep the English out of Tyrone and out of most of Ulster. In his later years, he was challenged by Hugh O'Neill, the then Baron of Dungannon, who was supported by the English. Tirlough Lynough had three sons - Sir Arthur, Henry and Cormac.

Sir Arthur, on the death of his father became the Queen's O'Neill. In opposition to the great Hugh O'Neill, Earl of Tyrone, he helped the English capture Lifford from O'Donnel. Sir Arthur had seven sons - Tirlough, Neil, Brian, Con, Cormac, Henry and Owen. At the plantation of Ulster, Tirlough, son of Sir Arthur O'Neill, received 3,300 acres of land in the Barony of Dungannon. His brother, Niel got 800 acres and Brian got 370 acres. They took part in the rebellion of 1641. Tirlough was a colonel in Owe Roe O'Neill's army. He was in Waterford with General Farrell.

By 1653, Tirlough had only 1,000 acres left of his grant of 3,000 acres in the plantation of Ulster. He was ordered to transplant to Connacht where he was to receive 400 acres.

The O'Neill's of Kinard (Calendon)

This branch of the O'Neill's are descended from Sean (John) O'Neill, second son of Con More O'Neill, Prince of Tyrone and a brother to Art Og O'Neill, prince from 1514 to 1519 and to Con Bacach O'Neill, who succeeded Art Og as Prince of Tyrone.

John was Art Og's Tanist and would have succeeded him as Prince if he had lived. John of Kinard was married and had a son, Henry, who had a son, Sir Henry Og, who was knighted by Queen Elizabeth for his disservice to his father-in-law, Hugh O'Neill, Earl of Tyrone.

Sir Henry did furnish the Earl of Tyrone with a rising out of 40 horse and 200 foot from his territory. Henry Og was in command of the company of 100 foot in Tyrone's army in 1600 A.D., but he went over to the English, who promised him his land, free of tribute to the Earl of Tyrone.

In 1607, after the flight of the Earls, Henry Og was assigned 2,000 acres of land in Kinard and 2,000 more in Oneilland, which was increased to 4,900 acres. Henry Og joined the English to crush Sir Cahir O'Doherty's rebellion, but he was killed in Donegal by O'Doherty, who raided his badly guarded camp.

At the same time, Henry's oldest son, Tirlough was so severely wounded that he only survived his father a short time. Tirlough was married to Kathleen O'Neill of the Fews family. They had two sons, Sir Phalem and Tirlough Og. Sir Phalem was an infant when his father died and the Dublin government felt it was undesirable to invest a large property in an infant, so they divided the property among Sir Phalem's uncles, leaving a reasonable share for Sir Phalem to inherit when he came of age.

Robert Hovendon married his mother and they undertook the charge of young Phalem. When Sir Phalem grew up, he became dissatisfied with the arrangement that gave his uncles property that should have belonged to him. Educated as a lawyer, he was successful in having it returned. In 1641, Sir Phalem became a national hero as the commander of the Ulster forces that captured most of the Engish strongholds in that province.

At the beginning of the 1641 revolution, having no military training, he relinquished his command to General Owen Roe O'Neill when he arrived in Ireland from Europe, but remained a colonel in Owen Roe's army until he surrendered the fort of Charlemont. In 1651, he was tried and executed by the English.

Sir Phalem was married three times— 1) to a daughter of Lord Iverah; 2) to General Preston's daughter and 3) to Lady Jane Gordon. She was the mother of Brigade General Gordon O'Neill of James II army, also in the French army. Sir Phalem's first wife was the mother of his son, Henry.

The O'Neill's of the Fews (In Armagh)

This branch of the O'Neill's were descended from Owen More, Prince of Tyrone from 1432 to 1455 A.D. Through Owen's second son, Hugh and whose son, Art O'Neill was Prince of Tyrone from 1509 to 1514. When Art died in 1514, he left two sons, Phalem Roe and Neil More. Phalem succeeded his father as Lord of the Fews, but not of Tyrone.

His son, Henry, surnamed Na Grathadh, i.e., of the cries, married Joan McGuire, the widow of Matthew, 1st Baron of Dungannon. Their son, Sir Tirlough O'Neill, was a half brother of Hugh O'Neill, Earl of Tyrone. He was the last elected Chief of the Fews.

During the Tyrone wars, Sir Tirlough opposed his half-brother, the Earl of Tyrone. After the flight of the Earl, the English government granted him 10,000 acres in the Fews. Two of his sons, Hugh Boy and Art received 250 each. Sir Tirlough died in 1639. His oldest son, Sir Henry of Glassdrummond received his estates. Sir Tirlough O'Neill also had three daughters. The oldest of them, Kathleen, was the wife of Sir Tirlough O'Neill of Kinard and the mother of Sir Phalem O'Neill, the leader of the 1641 rebillion.

Sir Henry O'Neill was married to Mary O'Reilly. They had two sons, Tirlough and Sean. Both of them took part in the 1641 wars. Tirlough was a colonel of a regiment of foot in Owen Roe O'Neill's army at the battle of Benburb. Tirlough and his regiment were part of the garrison of Clonmel, under General Hugh Dubb O'Neill that gave Cromwell his first setback in Ireland. At the conclusion of peace between Ormonde, Inchiquin and the confederate supreme council, he and several other colonels refused to back Owen Roe in his stand against the Lord Deputy

Ormonde. Tirlough was married to Cecilia, a daughter of Rory O'More of Ballyna, County Kildare. Tirlough's brother, Sean was a captain and later a colonel of horse in the Irish army.

After the war was over, Tirlough and his father, Henry were transplanted to the Barony of Gallen, County Mayo, where they received 2,600 acres at a Crown rent of 26 pounds, 9 shilings, 10 pence.

Tirlough left issue - a son, Henry, a captain in James II army. Henry was attained by the Williamite government. He was supposed to have escaped to the Continent. The estate then passed to Henry's cousin, Tirlough, son of Art, second son of Sir Tirlough of the Fews, whose son, Arthur had two sons, Neil and Owen. Neil was married to Catherine McGuinnis. Their son, Henry was under age in 1708 and still living in 1758 when John Knox of Moyne, County Mayo brought ejectment proceedings against him. The estate was called Oldcastle, not a great distance from Bonneconlon, County Mayo.

The Clanaboy O'Neill's

Hugh Boy O'Neill, from whom the Territory of Clanaboy takes its name, became King of Tyrone after Brian of Down was slain in 1260. He ruled Tyrone until 1283. His father was a first cousin of Brian of Down, which was the senior line. Hugh Boy O'Neill was a good soldier and was married to Eleanor DeAngelo. Her family later took the Irish name of MacCostello.

In 1264, Hugh Boy took title as King of all the Irish in Ireland. In 1272, he aided Henry DeMandeville in his fight against Fitzwain, the Ulster seneschal. In 1281, he defeated the O'Donnell's who had invaded Tyrone with a loss of 19 of O'Donnell's subchiefs. Henry was slain in 1283 by the McMahons when he invaded their territory as overlord.

After his death, his son, Brian claimed Tyrone until 1295 when he was slain by Donal, son of Brian of Down of the elder line at the battle of Coabbh Teleha.

Nevertheless, at the death of Donal in 1325, Henry, grandson of Hugh Boy O'Neill, succeeded as Prince of Tyrone until 1344, when he was expelled by Hugh of the senior line. Henry was the last of the Clanaboy O'Neill's to rule Tyrone. From then on the junior line was content to remain Chiefs of Clanaboy, which was later divided into two divisions - upper and lower Clanaboy. Often allied with the English at the Reformation in England under Henry VIII and Elizabeth, some of them became Protestants.

Clanaboy O'Neill's served in the 1641 war. One was Daniel O'Neill of upper Clanaboy, comprising the northeast portion of

County Down. His father, Con O'Neill served the English in the war against Hugh O'Neill, Earl of Tyrone. After the flight of the Earls, he received a grant of 66,000 acres, which he was induced to transfer to Sir Hugh Montgomery and James Hamilton for 60 pounds and a yearly rent of 160 pounds.

His son, Daniel, became a soldier in the Prince of Orange's army. Later he joined the English army and was accused of high treason. At the beginning of the fight for freedom in 1641, he was imprisoned in the Tower of London, but escaped after six months to Ireland. His mother was a sister of Owen Roe O'Neill. Daniel often acted as Owen Roe's ambassador. After his uncle's death, the Lord Lt. Ormonde tried to have him appointed commander of the Ulster army. His religion was against him as he was a Protestant. A bishop, Heber McMahon was elected instead, which was disastrous to the Ulster army.

In 1650, Daniel left Ireland with permission to transport 5,000 men to serve in the Spanish army. After the restoration of Charles II to the English Crown, Daniel was appointed Postmaster General. He died in 1664 of an ulcer of his stomach.

Colonel Con Og O'Neill was a brother of Daniel O'Neill. After some service with the Irish army, he was kiled at the battle of Clone, July, 1643, after quarter was given.

The Clanaboy O'Neill's

Colonel Sir Brian O'Neill of upper Clanaboy, became a soldier at an early age, serving under the Prince of Orange in Holland. He returned to Ireland before 1641 and received a commission in the Irish army. He was one of the officers Charles I communicated with. He joined the King's standard in England where he showed great bravery at the battle of Edge Hill for which he was created a Baronet.

Returning again to Ireland, he was appointed a colonel under Ormonde and was taken prisoner in 1647 by General Preson and was exchanged the next year for Captain Stephans. He was again taken prisoner by Colonel John Jones. He lived to see the restoration, dying in 1670.

By his first wife, he had one son. Sir Brian, who became Baron of the Exchequer and wrote a history of Ireland. By his second wife, Sarah, a daughter of Patrick Savage of Portaferry, he had a son, Hugh. Both brothers adhered to the cause of James II and lost what remained of the family estate.

Lt. Colonel Phalem McTool O'Neill was the grandfather of Col. Henry O'Neill, author of the relation and account of part of the war of 1641 from the Irish side. Phalem McTool O'Neill was a Lt. Colonel of General Owen Roe's regiment in the Ulster army. He commanded a part of the horse and musketeers amounting to 600 men at the battle of Benburb. Before that, he routed a large body of Scots who were raiding in County Down, killing 300 of them.

The Irish troops in Clanaboy in 1641 were commanded by Art Og O'Neill, Con Og O'Neill and Tool O'Neill. Sir Neil O'Neill, son of Sir Henry O'Neill of lower Clanaboy won fame in James II army at the battle of the Boyne. He was Colonel of a regiment of dragoons which he raised himself. At the head of his regiment, he charged three times through the river, beating back General Schomberg's best troops. He was wounded in the thigh and taken to Dublin and then to Waterford, where he died of his wounds. He was only 32 years old.

He was married and had five daughters. He was succeeded by his brother, Sir Daniel O'Neill. From him the family was carried down to a Mary O'Neill, who married the Rev. Arthur Chichester, a descendant of Sir Arthur Chichester who grew rich on the spoils taken from the native Irish during the plantation of Ulster. This Arthur Chichester's descendants assumed the name of O'Neill. One of them was Captain O'Neill, who was a Prime Minister of the six counties of Ulster during the early civil rights marches there until he was forced to resign by the militant Protestants in the area.

Colonel Felix O'Neill of that family went to Europe with James II, where he served as an officer of the Irish brigade. From him the O'Neill's of Portugal are descended.

O'Neill's Who Took Part
In the War of 1641

General Owen O'Neill, Colonel Sir Phalem O'Neill, Lt. Col. Sean Og O'Neill, Lt. General Brian McHugh Boy O'Neill, Colonel Tirlough O'Neill, McArt Og, Colonel Tirlough O'Neill of the Fews, Colonel Con Og O'Neill of Clanaboy, Colonel Brian O'Neill of Clanaboy, Captains Phalem O'Neill, Donal O'Neill, Tirlough O'Neill, Neil Og O'Neill, Cormac O'Neill, Donal O'Neill, Brian O'Neill, Tirlough McArt O'Neill, Sean O'Neill, Art McHugh O'Neill, Tirlough McShane O'Neill, Art O'Neill, Ever O'Neill, Brian McArt Og O'Neill, Henry McTool O'Neill.

O'Neill's Killed At the Battle of Scariffhollis

Major General Henry O'Neill, son of Owe Roe, hung by the English under Coote after he surrendered; Colonel Phalem McTool O'Neill; Lt. Colonel Phalem O'Neill, Adjutant General; Lt. Colonel Tirlough O'Neill; Major Phalem O'Neill; Captain Art Og O'Neill, Captain of Horse; Captain Brian O'Neill, Captain of Foot. Other O'Neill's killed during the war of 1641: Captain

Phalem O'Neill. the Grim; Captain Art Og O'Neill; Colonel Con Og O'Neill of Clanaboy; Captain Neil O'Neill and Captain Tirlough O'Neill of the Fews.

O'Neill's In King James II Army

Brigade General Gordon O'Neill; Tyrone. son of Sir Phalem O'Neill; Colonel Felix O'Neill, Clanaboy; Colonel Sir Niel O'Neill. Clanaboy; Colonel Cormac O'Neill; Major Henry O'Neill; Lt. Colonel Brian O'Neill; Colonel Con O'Neill and Captain Henry O'Neill.

O'Neill's Who Served With the Irish Brigade in France

Sir Major Henry O'Neill 1678
Colonel Gordon O'Neill 1697
Captain Con O'Neill 1697
Captain Con O'Neill 1708
Lt. Col. Eugene O'Neill 1708-22
Captain Neil O'Neill.. 1711
Ensign Gordon O'Neill 1690
Captain Gordon O'Neill.................................... 1718
Lt. Charles O'Neill... 1723
Captain Francois O'Neill............................... 1729
Captain Francois O'Neill.............................. 1741
Lt. Col. Jacques O'Neill.................................. 1761
Sous Lt. Felix O'Neill....................................... 1761
Captain Bernard O'Neill................................. 1777
Sous Lt. Henry O'Neill..................................... 1783
Sous Lt. John O'Neill 1783
Major Jean O'Neill.. 1783
Colonel Charles O'Neill 1821
Lt. Charles O'Neill.. 1800

O'Neill's Who Served France and Spain

Brigadier Gordon O'Neill, son of Sir Phalem O'Neill, one of the leaders of the 1641 rebellion in Ireland, by his third wife, Lady Jane Gordon, daughter of the Marquis of Huntley. Under James II, Gordon O'Neill was Lord Lt. and member of Parliament for Tyrone, also a captain of grenadiers in the Infantry regiment of Lord Mountjoy.

During the rebellion against James II in England, Gordon O'Neill raised a regiment of foot, mostly in Tyrone for service in James II army and carried out very successful operations against the Williamites in Ulster. Before the siege of Derry, he was at the blockade with the regiment that bore his name as the colonel. In 1690, he was at the battle of the Boyne and in 1691, he was a Brigadier General at the battle of Aughrim, where he was wounded and captured.

After the treaty of Limerick, Gordon O'Neill went to France where he was made a colonel of the Irish regiment of Charlemount. He was married and had one daughter, Catherine, who married John Burke, 4th Lord of Brittis and 9th Lord of Castle-Connell. They had two sons who were officers in the French army. Their father had to leave Ireland as a Jacobite loyalist. Brigadier General Gordon O'Neill died in France in 1704.

Brigadier John O'Neill was born in Derrynoose, County Armagh in 1727, went to France when he was very young and to College DeIrelaise near Paris where his brother was a principal. Finishing his studies at the College of Plessis, he then joined the regiment of Clare as a cadet, rising through the ranks to a Brigadier General.

He fought in the West India Islands against the English during the American Revolution against the English rule. He died in Paris in 1811. His son, **Colonel Charles O'Neill** was born in France in 1770. Entering the French army, he served under the Republic, the Empire and the restoration of the Bourbons. An officer of the Legion of Honor and a Chevalier of St. Louis Etc, he was appointed Chief of the Bureau of Infantry until the revolution of 1820. He died in 1844.

In Spain

The O'Neill family are represented by the **Marquise De La Granje**, De Valdeasera, De Caltojan and Conde De Bonajear, dating from 1679. Also in Spain was **Lt. General Carlos Felix O'Neill**, who died in 1791. He was a former Governor of Havana, Cuba and a great favorite of the King of Spain.

O'Neill's in America

One-hundred-seventy-eight O'Neill's served in George Washington's army during the American Revolution from British control.

O'Neill's who served in the Irish American Brigade included:

Captain B.S. O'Neill, 69th Regiment, New York Volunteers;
Captain J.O. O'Neill, 116th Regiment, Pennsylvania;
Captain John O'Neill, 116th Regiment, Pennsylvania;
Colonel Thomas O'Neill, Battery, Irish American Brigade;
Major Joseph O'Neill, 63rd New York Volunteers.

James O'Neill, actor, born in the Townland of Grennan

near Thomastown, County Limerick married Ella Quinlan in 1847. They came to American in 1850. He became a leading actor in America, winning fame as the Count of Monte Cristo in that popular play. he died in 1920. His son, **Eugene Gladstone O'Neill**, the American dramatist, was born in 1888 and began writing plays when he was twenty-seven years old. Eugene O'Neill's first stage success was *Bound East From Cardiff*. Others were a *Long Days Journey Into Night, Anna Christie, Marco Millions, Mourning Becomes Electra*, and *The Iceman Cometh*. A Nobel Prize Winner for Literature, he Nied November 27th, 1953.

Peggy O'Neill, a daughter of William O'Neill, a Washington saloon keeper, married John Henry Eaton, a lawyer and member of Andrew Jackson's Cabinet. Peggy was born in 1796 and died in 1879.

Colonel John O'Neill was born in Ulster, Ireland in 1834. He led the Fenian invasion of Canada in 1867. He died in 1878.

Edward Buffield O'Neill, United States author was born on August 9th, 1823 in Philadelphia, Pennsylvania. A Reformed Episcopal clergyman, he wrote *Treads of Maryland Colonial History* in 1867, the *History of the Virginia Company in London* in 1869 and the *English Colonization of American in the 17th Century*. He died September 26th, 1893.

Thomas P. O'Neill, Congressman from Massachusetts was born in Boston in 1912, a grandson of an emmigrant who left Ireland during the famine years. He became Speaker of the House of Representatives in December 1976, a position he still holds at the present time.

Other Well-Known O'Neill's

Francis O'Neill (1849-1936), folklorist, was born at Trailbane, County Cork first became a seaman, which permitted him to see the world. He immigrated to the United States in 1866. Seven years later, he 1873, he joined the Chicago police force. By 1901, he was their general superintendent. During the period he was superintendent. he contacted several Irish musicians, providing for them police jobs which gave them time to cultivate their music. O'Neill then began to publish several collections of traditional Irish airs, such as *The Music of Ireland, The Dance Music of Ireland, Gems of Irish Melody, Waifs and Strays of Irish Melody*. He wrote two books on the story of his experience collecting Irish folk music, Irish minstrels and musicians. He died in the U.S.A.

Henry O'Neill, archaeologist, was born in Dundalk, County Louth in 1800. He published two works which are highly esteemed by antiquaries, one *Sculptured Crosses of Ancient Ireland* in 1863, a brochure claiming Ireland for the Irish, and a description of the 12th Century Cross of Cong, a priceless reliquary of oak, copper and gold and made to enshine a portion of the True Cross. He died in Lower Gardiner Street, Dublin, on December 21st, 1880.

Hugh O'Neill, architectural draftsman, was born in Bloomsbury, London on April 20th, 1784, a son of an architect who designed a portion of Portland Place, London. The early part of his life was spent at Oxford, where he taught drawing. He lived for a time in Bath, then in Edinburgh and Bristol. While in Bristol, he made over 500 drawings. There are 15 of his pencil and water color drawings in the British Museum and three more in the South Kensington Museum. He died in poverty on April 7th, 1824 in Prince Street, Bristol.

Arthur O'Neill, the wandering blind harper, (1737-1816), was of the first in in the field of traditional music.

John O'Neill, the Temperance poet, was born in Waterford City in 1778. Some of his published works were *Mary of Avonmore, Irish Melodies, The Drunkard* (a poem), *The Blessing of Temperance, The Triumph of Temperance, Handerhan, the Irish Fairy Man,* and *The Legends of Carrick.* He died in 1860.

O'Neill Pedigree (No. 1)

Monarchs of Ireland, Kings of Ulster and Prices of Tyrone

Niall Mor H/K of Ireland, married Roigneach, British Princess (87).

Owen More, 1st King of Aileach, married (88).

Nutreadach, 2nd King of Aileach, married Earca, daughter of the King of Alba (89).

Their son, Muriartach More McEarca, 131st H/K of Ireland (90).

His son, Donal, 135th H/K of Ireland (91).

His son, Hugh, 143rd H/K of Ireland (92).

His son, Maolfreach, King of Aileach (93).

His son, Maoldoon, King of Aileach (Ulster) (94).

His son, Fargal, King of Aileach and 156th H/K of Ireland (95).

His son, Niall Frassach, King of Aileach and 162nd H/K (96).

His son, Hugh Ordnigh, 164th H/K of Ireland (97).

His son, Niall Caille, 166th H/K of Ireland (98).

His son, Hugh Finnliath, 168th H/K of Ireland (99).

Niall Glundubh, 170th H/K of Ireland. From this monarch, the surname O'Neill or Clan-na-Neill is derived. He was married to Gromlaight, daughter of High King Flan-Sionna. He was killed fighting the Danes near Dublin in 919 A.D. (100).

His son, Murchertach of the Leather Cloaks, King of Aileach (101).

His son, Donal of Armagh, 173rd H/K of Ireland (102).

His son, Moritach of Meath was the first that assumed the surname and title of the "Great O'Neill, Prince of Tyrone and of Ulster" (103).

His son, Flathartach An Frostain, Prince of Ulster (104).

His son, Hugh Athlanh, Prince of Tyrone (105).

His son, Donal An Togdhamh, Prince of Tyrone (106).

His son, Flahertach Locha Hadha, Prince of Tyrone (107).

His son, Connor of the Woods, Prince of Tyrone (108).

His son, Teige Glinne, Prince of Tyrone (109).

His son, Mortogh Muighe Line, Prince of Ulster (110).

His son, Hugh An Macaomh Toinleasg, Prince of Tyrone and Ulster (111).

He had two sons, Niall Ruadh and Hugh Dubh (112).

The O'Neills of Tyrone and the Fews are from the line of Niall Raudh (Red). The Clanaboy O'Neills are descended from his brother, Hugh Dubh.

O'Neill Pedigree (No. 2)
The O'Neill Kings of Cinel Eoghain (Tyrone)

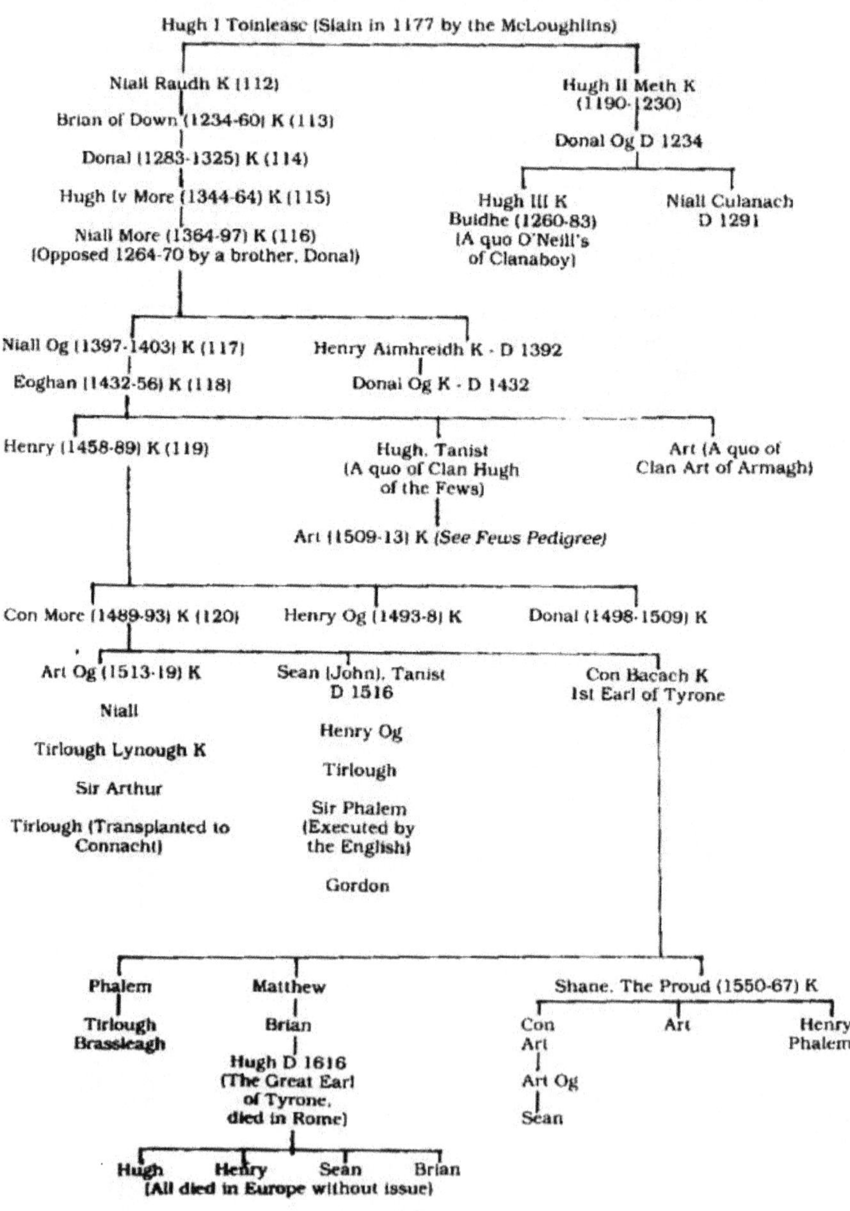

Pedigree of the O'Neill's of the Fews

Hugh O'Neill, second son of Owen, Prince of Tyrone, was the Lord of the Fews.

His son, Art, was Prince of Tyrone from 1509 to 1514.

His son, Phalem Raudh, Lord of the Fews.

His son, Henry, Lord of the Fews.

His son, Sir Tirlough, married Sarah, a daughter of Tirlough Lynough O'Neill.

His son, Henry, married Mary O'Reilly. He was transplanted to Connacht.

His son, Tirlough, was a Colonel in Owen Roe O'Neill's army. He fought against Cromwell at Clonmel. He was transplanted with his father, Henry to Oldcastle near Foxford, County Mayo.

His son, Con, was also transplanted to County Mayo.

His son, Henry, was a Captain in James II army. In 1689, he was supposed to have excaped to France. The Estate then went to his cousin,

Niall O'Neill of Clone, County Leitrim.

His son, Henry O'Neill of Carrowrony was under age in 1718 and still living in 1758, when John Knox of Moyne, County Mayo, brought ejectment proceedings against him.

O'Neill's of Clanaboy Pedigree

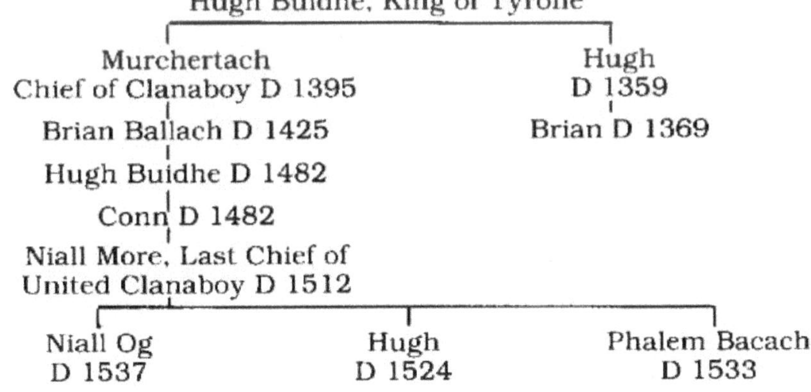

The O'Neill's of Ulster belong to the oldest traceable family left in Europe. Their ancestry goes back to Heremon. He was the first Milesian absolute monarch of Ireland. The name is derived from Niall, which means champion in Irish. Dohnall O'Neill, High King of Ireland, was the first to introduce surnames, when he prefixed O (descending from) to the name of his grandfather, Niall Glundubh, also a High King who was slain in battle with the Danes in 919 A.D.

There are roughly 29,000 O'Neills in Ireland and over 30,000 O'Neill families live in the United States, with many more thousands scattered throughout the world.

Besides the Ulster O'Neills, there are three other distinct O'Neill families in Ireland. (1) The O'Neills of Thomond, who are of Delcassian origin, were Chiefs of a territory called Clan Dealbuidhe in County Clare. The O'Nihills of Clare and Creaghs of Clare and Limerick are of the same family.

(2) The Leinster O'Neills of Rathvilly, County Carlow and Shillelagh, County Wicklow, an ancient family, who were Chiefs of a large district in the above Counties. Eliza O'Neill, one of Ireland's greatest actresses was of that family and Henry O'Neill, the well known archaeologist. Two of his works were *The Most Interesting of the Sculptured Crosses of Ancient Ireland* and *The Fine Arts and Civilizations of Ancient Ireland*. He died in Dublin in 1880 in poor circumstances, having spent all his money in the productions of his works.

(3) The O'Neills of Munster of South Tipperary and East Waterford. The O'Neills of Ballyneill near Carrick-on-Suir had estates there up until the 17th century when they were dispossessed by Comwell. One of that family, Hugh O'Neill was a leader in the 1798 revolution. He escaped from the battle of Vinegar Hill and fled to France.

There are O'Neill families in Connacht, who are really Ulster O'Neills, descendants of the few Ulster O'Neills who owned land there before the 1641 revolution. They were all transplanted into Connacht.

The writer is of the Fews family, a branch of the Tyrone O'Neills.